Uniform System of Financial Reporting for Clubs

Uniform System of Financial Reporting for Clubs

Sixth Revised Edition

Club Managers Association of America, Inc.
Alexandria, Virginia

Hospitality Financial and Technology Professionals
Austin, Texas

Educational Institute
American Hotel & Lodging Association
Orlando, Florida

Disclaimer

This publication is designed to provide accurate and authoritative information in regard to the subject matter covered. It is sold with the understanding that the publisher is not engaged in rendering legal, accounting, or other professional service. If legal advice or other expert assistance is required, the services of a competent professional person should be sought.

> —*From the Declaration of Principles jointly adopted by the American Bar Association and a Committee of Publishers and Associations.*

Nothing contained in this publication shall constitute a standard, an endorsement, or a recommendation of the Educational Institute or the American Hotel & Lodging Association (AH&LA). The Institute and AH&LA disclaim any liability with respect to the use of any information, procedure, or product, or reliance thereon by any member of the hospitality industry.

Hospitality Financial and Technology Professionals

A few words from the sponsor of this edition of the *Uniform System of Financial Reporting for Clubs*

Hospitality Financial and Technology Professionals is the international society for financial and technology professionals in the hospitality industry. Serving the industry since 1953, HFTP provides outstanding educational programs, networking opportunities, and information resources to hospitality professionals around the world. HFTP also awards the Certified Hospitality Accountant Executive (CHAE) and Certified Hospitality Technology Professional (CHTP) designations.

The goal of HFTP is to be recognized by the global business community as the authoritative information source on finance and technology for the hospitality industry. We are reaching that goal through the following.

Invaluable Resources

- *www.hftp.org.* The HFTP web site provides members with convenient access to industry checklists, forms, and tips; streaming video and audio educational sessions; CHAE and CHTP reviews; online meeting registration; publication archives; Job Mart; membership directory and ability for members to update their profiles; and resources for chapter leaders.

- *The Bottomline.* Produced eight times a year, HFTP's professional journal provides members with industry news covering everything from taxes and technology to HR and accounting issues.

- *Infoline.* HFTP's bimonthly newsletter notifies members of association activities on both the local and international levels, providing well-deserved recognition to chapters and individual members for their contributions to the hospitality industry.

- *Industry Partnerships.* We pride ourselves on enhancing the image of financial and technology professionals through increased visibility, support, and networking in the hospitality industry. HFTP represents members at industry meetings and associations, and has collaborated with other organizations to conduct industry research in the areas of hospitality salaries, technology, capital, and e-business.

Education and Technology

- *HITEC (Hospitality Industry Technology Exposition and Conference): www. hitec.org.* Internationally known, this conference offers industry professionals the largest, most comprehensive coverage of hospitality technology of its kind in the world. HITEC offers live demonstrations of the latest in hospitality technology, equipment, products and services, first-rate educational programs, and networking.

- *Annual Convention & Tradeshow.* More than 600 members attend the Annual Convention & Tradeshow each year to participate in information-sharing, educational sessions, and fun-filled entertainment.

- *Professional Development Seminars.* Each year, a series of specialized educational opportunities are offered to various segments of the hospitality industry, including the Club Controllers Conference, Hotel Controllers Conference, and Casino Controllers Conference.

- *Online Master's Program.* HFTP has collaborated with the University of Nevada Las Vegas to provide an online master's degree in hospitality administration (finance or technology concentration). HFTP members are eligible for tuition discounts.

Professional Opportunities

- *Certification.* The Certified Hospitality Accountant Executive (CHAE) designation is recognized worldwide as a symbol of achievement and competence. The Certified Hospitality Technology Professional (CHTP) designation—co-sponsored with the Educational Institute—symbolizes a high level of competency and professionalism in hospitality technology. Individuals who earn these designations are respected by employers and colleagues for their high level of commitment and dedication.

- *Networking.* The Colleague Advisory Network connects members who have expressed experience on particular subjects with members who have questions in that area. In addition, local chapters around the world provide members with leadership opportunities, discussion forums, and social activities.

For more information, contact HFTP at 11709 Boulder Lane, Ste. 110, Austin, TX 78726, membership@hftp.org, 800-646-4387, fax: 512-249-1533, or visit www.hftp.org and www.hitec.org.

Contents

APPENDICES

Preface

A club is a cooperative association of members with a common interest who band together to share the cost of providing and maintaining social and recreational facilities. The importance of clubs in the social life of our nation has long been recognized. With the ever-rising standards of living in this country, the number of clubs is steadily expanding.

It is said all clubs are different. True, each attracts a slightly different membership, each has its own atmosphere, and many different economic levels are evident. But, diverse though clubs may be in these respects, at the core of all club operations is dues income, imposed to share the cost of providing recreational clubhouse facilities, the club's major reason for existence.

A consistent relationship between income and expenses is just as essential in club operations as in any other business. Club managers and officers are aware that when operating statistics of a club are available in a form sufficiently standardized for ready comparison with other clubs, the use of such comparisons can assist management to achieve the best operating results and provide a sound financial structure to withstand changing economic conditions.

This book represents more than eight decades of development in establishing a common language for club accounting. Although written specifically to cover country and city club operations, minor variations in terminology will make it equally acceptable for yacht, beach, tennis, riding, and other types of clubs.

The ideas on which the system was originally based were contributed by club managers and accounting firms specializing in this field. A few words on the history of this book are in order.

An attempt was made to standardize the accounting systems of country clubs as early as 1915 by the Chicago District Golf Association, which in 1918 published a booklet entitled *Standardized Accounting System for Country Clubs*. During the same period, work was being done on uniform systems for other industries. Among the most successful systems developed were the *Uniform System of Accounts for Hotels* (1926) and a system of standardized accounts for restaurants (1927). The ideas evolved by these systems were used as far as practicable in the suggested classification of accounts for country clubs and city clubs that were to follow shortly.

The Club Managers Association of America was founded in 1927 and elected Colonel C. G. Holden and Frank H. Murray as the first president and secretary, respectively. By 1932, these two gentlemen prepared a draft of the Suggested Classification of Accounts for Country Clubs. This material was reviewed and arranged for publication by Horwath & Horwath. Nearly a decade passed before a similar booklet appeared for city clubs. Harry J. Fawcett was CMAA President in 1941, and enlisted the cooperation of John N. Horwath and George Podd of Horwath & Horwath in this undertaking. Thinking wider acceptance might accrue if this work were credited to actual club managers, they had the manuscript reviewed by a committee of well-known managers: Martin Henkel, E. Park Akin, and George Jobe, the latter two being CMAA directors. The resulting booklet was entitled *Proposed Uniform System of Accounts for City Clubs* and presented to CMAA for copyright during its 1942 convention as a closing gesture of Mr. Fawcett's presidency. Only a relatively few mimeographed copies of the original edition were published. A rerun was scheduled, but our entry into World War II channeled energies elsewhere and nothing further was done.

A decade later, Thomas C. McGaffey, Chairman of the Educational Committee, reported to the CMAA Board that the firm of Horwath & Horwath was prepared to draw up and present copy for two standardized accounting booklets, one for country clubs and the other for town clubs. The project took two years, by which time it was decided to combine the two works as sections under one cover. It was entitled *Uniform System of Accounts for Clubs* and was first presented for sale at the 1954 CMAA Conference.

The breadth of this book's acceptance exhausted the supply of texts in just over half the anticipated period.

In 1960, CMAA President Kenneth Meisnet appointed an ad hoc Uniform System Revision Committee to review and recommend changes to the 1954 edition. This committee was composed of a country club manager, Forest Davis of Connecticut; a city club manager, Richard Kirwan of New York; and two CPAs whose firms specialized in club accounting, Joseph Nolin of Horwath & Horwath and Arthur Iredell of Harris, Kerr Forster & Company (now PKF). Philip Stone of New York was designated chairman. The committee's task was accomplished with the publication of the First Revision in 1960 and the committee was dissolved.

In 1965, the committee was reactivated. Mr. Stone was again called upon to chair the committee and the committeemen were CMAA members Henry Ogden Barbour, Jr., William Conner, Joseph J. Donoghue, CCM, and Laurice T. Hall, CCM. In 1966, the committee was further expanded to include Whitney Travis, CCM, a vice-chairman, and Lloyd G. Weber, CCM. Messrs. Iredell and Nolin continued in an advisory capacity. This committee updated the publication and issued the second revised edition in 1967.

Thirteen years elapsed before the CMAA Board of Directors requested that the third revised edition be published. The committee charged with effecting the update comprised Chairman Clarence C. Watson, CCM; John J. Black; Robert M. Broms, CCM; Paul C. Frederick; and Frederick E. Shaner, CCM. The committee was ably assisted by John P. Jaeger, CPA, of Pannell Kerr Forster, who provided technical advice and whose firm provided many hours of typing and organization of copy. The third revised edition was published in 1982.

In 1989, the CMAA Board of Directors requested that the fourth revised edition be published. The committee charged with this task consisted of Chairman Brian Spaulding, CCM; Carl Bauer, CCM; Michael Carabine; Robert James, CCM; George Poole, CCM; and Roger Ross, CCM. Patrick J. O'Meara of Pannell Kerr Forster served as the advisor to the committee and donated many hours of his time to coordinating and completing this project.

In 1994, due to a number of changes in the professional literature, the CMAA Board of Directors requested that a fifth revised edition be published. During the drafting process, it became clearer that the book dealt with more than the uniform system of accounts but rather with the total financial reporting of a club. The uniform system was merely the first step in establishing consistency in reporting. The committee charged with this responsibility consisted of William (Skip) Harris, CCM, Chairman; Albert Armstrong, CCM; John Billé; Patricia Dinger; William Shonk, CCM; Robert Spindel, CCM; and Dianne Vogel. Michael F. Moore, CPA, and Kevin F. Reilly, CPA, both of Pannell Kerr Forster, served as technical advisors to the committee and donated innumerable hours to coordinating and editing this edition; their firm also provided the secretarial and organizational support needed. Karen Miller of CMAA headquarters ably served as staff support and ensured that the committee stayed on task.

In 2001, the Boards of Directors of both CMAA and the Hospitality Financial and Technology Professionals requested that a sixth revised edition be published. In addition to updating statements and schedules, the committee formed for this revision has chosen to include an expense dictionary, an extensive uniform account numbering system, and illustrated financial statements. The revision committee consisted of three subcommittee chairs and the coordinator. The subcommittees were as follows:

Club Managers	Controllers	Consultants
Ian D. N. Fetigan, CCM (Chair)	Wendy K. Zurstadt, CPA, CHAE, CHTP (Chair)	Leonard J. Bartello, CPA, CHAE, CHTP (Chair)
Gavin J. Arsenault, CCM	Katherine Cavanagh, CHAE	Edward J. McGinty, CPA
Brian R. Kroh, CCM	Nabil M. Fahmy	Philip G. Newman, CPA
Pasquale J. LaRocca, CCM	David M. Manglos, CPA, CHAE	Robert M. Patasnick, CPA
Jay DiPietro, CCM	Andrew Moderski, CHAE	Kevin F. Reilly, CPA
Richard P. Smetana, CCM	Jerilyn B. Schnitzel, CHAE, CHTP	Mitchell L. Stump, CPA

Committee Coordinator: Raymond S. Schmidgall, CPA, CHAE

Although this edition is copyrighted by the Club Managers Association of America, it is to be credited to the efforts of all of the individual committee members and advisors mentioned in this history. CMAA and HFTP are indebted to them for their dedication.

Committee Report

To the Boards of Directors
Club Managers Association of America
Hospitality Financial and Technology Professionals

In order to update and expand the recommended standards for financial reporting by clubs, you have requested we revise the *Uniform System of Financial Reporting for Clubs*. Several of the changes in this edition from the prior edition are as follows:

- Several department schedules have been added including entertainment, golf shop, racquet shop, locker rooms, and telecommunications.

- The titles of some departmental schedules have been revised to reflect current usage, such as aquatic sports for swimming pool and facility maintenance for repairs and maintenance.

- Facility maintenance has been shown on the Statement of Activities as a separate activity. The Committee believes this treatment further emphasizes the importance of maintaining a club's facilities.

- For *internal* purposes, food minimum charges are shown as other revenue on the food department schedule. The Committee believes this reflects the reality of the club industry. For *external* purposes, food minimum charges continue to be shown as a separate revenue item as in the prior edition.

- Most statement of financial position line items are defined, as are the details of each departmental schedule. The Committee believes these descriptions provide needed guidance to users of this system.

- The uniform account numbering system has been greatly expanded to provide guidance to users.

- The illustrated statements and schedules section has been expanded. The illustration is developed starting with an adjusted trial balance of a hypothetical country club with a 18-hole golf course.

- An expense dictionary has been added to this edition of the Uniform System. The Committee believes this section will provide guidance to accounting personnel enabling greater compliance with this uniform system.

- This edition includes a broad discussion of tax issues to provide guidance primarily for planning purposes.

We appreciate the opportunity to be of service to both the Club Managers Association of America and the Hospitality Financial and Technology Professionals.

Respectfully submitted,

Raymond S. Schmidgall, CPA, CHAE, Chair
Leonard S. Bartello, CPA, CHAE, CHTP
Ian D. N. Fetigan, CCM
Wendy Zurstadt, CPA, CHAE, CHTP

Section 1
Basic Financial Statements

The financial statements of a club are the result of the accounting process. To be complete, the financial statements must include a statement of financial position (balance sheet), a statement of activities (income statement), a statement of cash flows, and any and all disclosures necessary to comply with generally accepted accounting principles.

An illustrative set of financial statements is presented in this section. These statements are presented for guidance only, since the accounts shown will not necessarily conform in all respects to the requirements of every club. A particular club may need to make certain minor modifications.

Some clubs are member-owned and the member-owners do not seek a financial return on their investments (not-for-profit organizations). Other clubs are owned by investors who ultimately do expect a financial reward from their ownership (for-profit organizations). The statements of activities and departmental schedules in the following sections are equally applicable to for-profit and not-for-profit clubs. The multi-column presentation of the statement of activities on page 15 may be the best presentation for a for-profit club that has a contractual obligation to the members to use initiation fees for replacement and improvements to property and equipment. The most significant difference between the financial statements of a for-profit and a not-for-profit club is in the owners' equity section of the statement of financial position. Because of the varied types of ownership vehicles of for-profit clubs (corporations, partnerships, etc.) and the voluminous amount of accounting literature that covers the financial presentation of the owners' equity of for-profit enterprises, *the following examples are for member-owned, not-for-profit clubs.*

The statement of financial position and the statement of cash flows can be used as guides for both city and country clubs. Separate statements of activities are presented for city clubs and for country clubs. Luncheon clubs can use the city club format as a guide, while beach clubs, yacht clubs, etc. can use the country club format.

The accounting presentation and disclosure in each set of financial statements should include what is needed in the particular circumstances for an informative presentation and should conform, in all material respects, with pronouncements of recognized financial and accounting authorities.

STATEMENT OF FINANCIAL POSITION
(BALANCE SHEET)

The Statement of Financial Position presentation can be used for both city clubs and country clubs and is similar to the balance sheet of a commercial enterprise. Naturally, the accounts as illustrated will not conform in all details to the requirements of each individual club, and minor modifications will be necessary to meet individual requirements.

Exhibit A

STATEMENT OF FINANCIAL POSITION
(Insert period ended)
Assets

	Current Year	Prior Year
CURRENT ASSETS		
Cash and cash equivalents	$	$
Short-term investments		
Receivables:		
Accounts receivable—members		
Notes and deferred initiation fees receivable		
Current portion of noncurrent receivables		
Other receivables		
Total receivables	_____	_____
Less allowance for doubtful accounts		
Net receivables	_____	_____
Inventories		
Prepaid expenses		
Other current assets	_____	_____
Total current assets	_____	_____
NONCURRENT RECEIVABLES, NET OF CURRENT PORTION		
DESIGNATED ASSETS		
INVESTMENTS—LONG-TERM		
PROPERTY AND EQUIPMENT		
Land		
Golf course and golf course improvements		
Construction in progress		
Leasehold and leasehold improvements		
Buildings and building improvements		
Furniture, fixtures, and equipment		
China, glassware, silver, linen, and uniforms		
Total property and equipment	_____	_____
Less accumulated depreciation and amortization	_____	_____
Net property and equipment	_____	_____
OTHER ASSETS		
Security deposits		
Deferred charges		
Other	_____	_____
Total other assets	_____	_____
TOTAL ASSETS	$ _____	$ _____

Exhibit A *(continued)*

STATEMENT OF FINANCIAL POSITION
(Insert period ended)
Liabilities and Net Assets

	Current Year	Prior Year
CURRENT LIABILITIES		
Notes payable	$	$
Accounts payable		
Taxes payable and accrued		
Accrued expenses		
Current portion of long-term debt		
Deferred revenue		
Deferred income taxes—current		
Special purpose funds		
Other current liabilities	_____	_____
Total current liabilities	_____	_____
LONG-TERM DEBT		
Notes payable, net of current maturity		
Obligations under capital lease, net of current maturity		
Mortgage payable, net of current maturity	_____	_____
Total long-term debt	_____	_____
OTHER LONG-TERM LIABILITIES		
Deferred compensation		
Deferred income taxes—noncurrent		
Interest rate swaps		
Other	_____	_____
Total other long-term liabilities	_____	_____
Total liabilities	_____	_____
UNRESTRICTED NET ASSETS (MEMBERS' EQUITY)		
Capital stock		
Designated		
Undesignated	_____	_____
Total unrestricted net assets	_____	_____
TOTAL LIABILITIES AND NET UNRESTRICTED ASSETS	$ _____	$ _____

ASSETS

Current Assets

Current assets represent accounts that can be converted to cash or used in operations within 12 months of the Statement of Financial Position date.

Cash and Cash Equivalents

Cash on hand (petty cash, house banks) and cash held in bank accounts is reflected in this line item. Any cash deposits at financial institutions with a maturity date less than 90 days from date of purchase would also be included here. An example might be a Certificate of Deposit or a Treasury issue.

Short-Term Investments

This line item contains investments intended to be converted to cash or cash equivalents within one year of the statement date. These investments should be presented at fair market value with the unrealized gain or loss recorded on the Statement of Activities. The notes to the financial statements should disclose the basis for valuation.

Receivables

Receivables can be reported as one total with a supplementary schedule detailing the items, or presented individually.

- *Accounts receivable—members* consists of the total amount due to the club on the members' open accounts for dues, assessments, and member charges.

- *Notes and deferred initiation fees receivable* refers to the total of these items that is to be collected within one year. Notes receivable from members and employees, if significant, should be shown separately.

- *Current portion of noncurrent receivables* refers to those receivables due within one year when the balance of the receivable would be recorded in noncurrent assets. If a club has a receivable that is expected to be collected within 18 months of the statement date, 12 months would be in the current assets and six months in the noncurrent assets.

- *Other receivables* refers to any receivables not addressed in the foregoing. Examples could include interest receivable and reciprocal club receivable.

Allowance for Doubtful Accounts

An allowance should be provided for the portion of accounts and notes receivable estimated to be uncollectible. Such provision should be based on historical experience, specific appraisal of individual accounts, or other accepted methods. Write-offs of accounts that prove uncollectible are charged to this account.

Inventories

The cost of merchandise held for sale, such as food and beverage, is included under this line item. The basis for valuation of the inventories should be disclosed in the financial statements. Inventory cost may be presented as one total. However, if the individual categories are significant in amount, they should be separately stated.

Prepaid Expenses

Expenditures made that are applicable to subsequent periods should be included under this line item. The expenditures are charged off to operations over the periods in which the benefit is received. Examples are insurance, property taxes, rent, supplies, and china, glassware, etc. Significant items might be stated separately on the Statement of Financial Position.

Other Current Assets

Other items expected to be realized in cash or consumed within one year are included under this line item. An example would be a mortgage escrow deposit.

Noncurrent Receivables

Accounts and notes receivable that are not due within one year are included under this line item. If any noncurrent receivables are considered to be uncollectible, an appropriate allowance for doubtful accounts should be recorded, similar to that used for current receivables.

Designated Assets

This line item includes cash, receivables, and investments that have been designated for special purposes.

Investments—Long-Term

This line item includes debt or equity instruments, regardless of whether they are traded in recognized markets, that are expected to be held for a period of more than one year. Investments should be reflected at market value. All unrealized gains and losses should be shown on the Statement of Activities. This item also includes certain deferred compensation where the ownership is retained by the club. If significant, this may be shown as a separate item on the Statement of Financial Position.

Property and Equipment

This section includes land, golf course and golf course improvements, construction in progress, leasehold and leasehold improvements, buildings and building improvements, furniture, fixtures, and equipment, and china, glassware, silver, linen, and uniforms. These items should be recorded at cost. There are different methods to account for china, glassware, and silver. The recommended method is to capitalize the initial cost of acquisition. This cost should be depreciated over a period of three years or less. Replacements are expensed when placed in service. Reserve stock would be recorded as prepaid expense.

Accumulated depreciation and amortization should be shown as a separate line item. The difference between total property and equipment and accumulated depreciation is the net property and equipment.

The methods of depreciation and amortization must be disclosed in the notes to the financial statements. Since most not-for-profit clubs are not pressured to earn high profits, the straight-line depreciation method may be preferable. It is recommended that clubs record depreciation on their internal financials to more accurately present the value of their property and equipment.

Other Assets

Security Deposits

Security deposits on property and equipment are included in this account.

Deferred Charges

This account consists of charges for goods or services received that are expected to benefit periods more than 12 months beyond the Statement of Financial Position date. Financing charges relating to the issuance of bonds, mortgages, or other forms of debt would also be included under this caption and amortized over the life of the issue.

Other

Items that cannot be included under other specific groupings are shown under this caption. An example would be the cash surrender value of life insurance.

LIABILITIES AND NET ASSETS

Current Liabilities

Current liabilities represent existing accounts at the Statement of Financial Position date that require satisfaction within 12 months.

Notes Payable

This line item includes short-term notes payable within the next 12 months. This would include notes to banks as well as other creditors.

Accounts Payable

Amounts due creditors for the purchase of all provisions, supplies, equipment, and services are included in this line item.

Taxes Payable and Accrued

All taxes payable and accrued, including payroll taxes withheld but not paid as of the financial closing date, unemployment taxes, property taxes, sales taxes, excise taxes, and any federal or state income taxes payable are included here.

Accrued Expenses

Any amounts incurred but not payable until after the financial closing date would be recorded here. Examples are salaries, wages, vacation pay, benefits, interest, rent, and utilities.

Current Portion of Long-Term Debt

This item includes the principal payments on outstanding mortgages, other notes due within the next 12 months, and the current installments on capital lease obligations.

Deferred Revenue

This item includes revenues received in advance that benefit future periods within the next 12 months, such as advance deposits, dues, and initiation fees.

Deferred Income Taxes—Current

This item reveals any tax effects resulting from temporary differences between financial and tax reporting for current items. For instance, a transaction recognized in the financial statements before it is required to be reported as a taxable item results in a deferred income tax.

Special Purpose Funds

May also be known as activity funds, prize funds, association funds, and pro shop credits and gift certificates. These funds are supported by members for tournaments and special events. The club maintains the recordkeeping only.

Other Current Liabilities

This item is used to record other minor liabilities not shown separately on the financial statement. Examples of this include food and other minimums received in advance.

Long-Term Debt

This category includes all the mortgage notes, promissory notes, obligations under capital leases, and similar liabilities that are not payable within the next 12 months. They represent the balance of the total obligation less the current period shown above.

Other Long-Term Liabilities

Liabilities that will not require satisfaction within the next 12 months and are not separately disclosed would be included in this category. Examples would be deferred compensation, deferred income taxes, and interest rate swaps.

Deferred Compensation

Deferred compensation arrangements are a common employee remuneration vehicle at many clubs. Such arrangements can take a number of forms, each one requiring different accounting treatment. The club should always consult with its professional accounting advisors before entering deferred compensation agreements to ensure that club management and the board fully understand the financial reporting impact. Deferred compensation arrangements can include, but are not limited to:

- Section 457 plans where the club will typically record an asset and liability of equal amount. Investments in such plans should be recorded at fair market value.

- One-time grants to specific employees for retirement benefits. Often, the board will decide to pay a long-time employee, upon retirement, a fixed sum for the remainder of his or her life or for a specified period. The present value of the payments should be recorded as a liability at the date the benefits are granted.

- Liabilities that will accrue to specific employees over a period of service. This type of deferred compensation arrangement is often buried in employment contracts of key personnel. Typically, the retirement benefit will vest over time and a liability should be accrued each period to record the vested amount.

None of these examples should be equivalent to a pension plan, as defined under GAAP.

Where a club has a plan to provide post-retirement benefits (typically health-care) to covered employees, an actuarial valuation of the plan may be required and a liability may need to be recorded.

Again, all of the above situations should be discussed with professional advisors prior to their enactment.

Deferred Income Taxes—Noncurrent

This item represents the tax effects of temporary differences between the bases of noncurrent assets and noncurrent liabilities for financial and income tax reporting purposes. For example, the use of accelerated depreciation for tax purposes and straight-line depreciation for financial reporting purposes will result in noncurrent deferred income taxes. Noncurrent deferred income taxes are presented as net noncurrent assets or net noncurrent liabilities as circumstances dictate.

Interest Rate Swaps

Clubs sometimes hedge the interest rate exposure on their variable-rate mortgages by entering into interest rate swap agreements. The result of such agreements fixes the effective interest rate paid by the club over the term of the swap agreement. Interest rate swap agreements typically are considered derivative financial instruments under Statement of Financial Accounting Standards No. 133. Clubs are required to record an asset or liability, depending on interest rate levels, on their Statement of Financial Position for the fair market value of the swap. The club should always consult with its professional accounting advisors before entering interest rate swap or other derivative agreements to ensure the financial reporting impact is fully understood by club management and the board.

Other

Examples of additional other long-term liabilities include advance deposits that will benefit the club more than 12 months from the Statement of Financial Position date, outstanding obligations to members, and accrued pension obligations.

Unrestricted Net Assets (Members' Equity)

The equity section is presented differently based on the type of club ownership. For corporations, the common term is Stockholders' Equity; for member-owned clubs, the common term is Members' Equity. FASB statement 117 requires that not-for-profit clubs present the equity section as Unrestricted Net Assets in external financial statements. However, the components would be similar.

- Capital stock (membership certificates)
- Designated net assets as determined by the board for specific purposes
- Undesignated net assets that are generated from normal operations

The equity section can be presented in summary form on the Statement of Financial Position and in a detailed statement presented separately.

STATEMENT OF ACTIVITIES

(INCOME STATEMENT)

The Statements of Activities for both city clubs and country clubs are commonly shown in two formats. One format (reflecting the total revenue and expenses) should be used in the financial statements because it is simple and more readily understood by the members. The other format (reflecting departmental operations) is usually preferred by management. The second format is presented in Section II.

The first format (shown as Exhibits B-1 and B-2) reflects the revenue from membership dues and fees and lists separately the total revenues of the major operating departments. The expenses of the various departments are listed under operating expenses. Finally, the fixed charges are summarized by category.

Occasionally, there may be significant infrequent items of income or expense (such as gain or loss from the sale of property). Such items should be shown immediately preceding provision for income taxes, if any, on the Statement of Activities.

The illustrative statements reflect depreciation as a fixed charge and do not allocate to each department. While some clubs allocate depreciation among departments to more accurately reflect the cost of the department, it may not be practicable for many clubs to allocate depreciation.

Another issue on which clubs have a variety of treatments is the classification of unused food minimum. It is recommended that such income be treated as other revenue after cost of sales is determined.

Initiation fees are treated as operating revenue if used for normal operations. If initiation fees are designated for capital improvements or for any other purpose, they should be included under the other activities section on the Statement of Activities. In all cases, initiation fees must be included in this statement.

An example of a Statement of Activities for a city club is presented as Exhibit B-1. An example for a country club is presented as Exhibit B-2.

As mentioned above, many clubs choose to designate certain sources of support, such as member assessments and initiation fees, as being reserved to fund the replacement of property and equipment or for other designated purposes. Exhibit B-3 presents an optional fund accounting presentation for such designated funds.

Exhibit B-1

CITY CLUB
STATEMENT OF ACTIVITIES
(External)

	Period Ended
REVENUE	
Membership dues	$
Initiation fees	
Unused food and other minimums	
Food	
Beverage	
Entertainment	
Overnight rooms	
Health and fitness	
Telecommunications	
Other operating departments	
Rentals and other revenue	_____
Total revenue	_____
OPERATING EXPENSES	
Overnight rooms	
Food	
Beverage	
Entertainment	
Health and fitness	
Telecommunications	
Other operating departments	
Clubhouse	
Administrative and general	
Facility maintenance	
Energy costs	_____
Total operating expenses	_____
INCOME BEFORE FIXED CHARGES	_____
FIXED CHARGES	
Rent	
Property taxes and other municipal charges	
Insurance	
Interest	
Depreciation and amortization	_____
Total fixed charges	_____
INCOME (LOSS) BEFORE TAXES	_____
PROVISION FOR INCOME TAXES	_____
Results of operations	_____
OTHER ACTIVITIES	
Initiation fees	
Special assessments	
Investment income	
Other	
INCREASE (DECREASE) IN UNRESTRICTED NET ASSETS (MEMBERS' EQUITY)	
UNRESTRICTED NET ASSETS, BEGINNING OF PERIOD	_____
UNRESTRICTED NET ASSETS, END OF PERIOD	$ _____

See notes to financial statements

Exhibit B-2

**COUNTRY CLUB
STATEMENT OF ACTIVITIES**
(External)

Period Ended

REVENUE
Membership dues $
Initiation fees
Unused food minimums
Food
Beverage
Entertainment
Golf operations
Golf shop
Racquet sports
Aquatic sports
Other sports activities
Overnight rooms
Locker rooms
Telecommunications
Other operating departments
Rentals and other revenue   _____
    Total revenue   _____

OPERATING EXPENSES
Food
Beverage
Entertainment
Golf operations
Golf shop
Golf course maintenance
Racquet sports
Racquet shop
Aquatic sports
Other sports activities
Overnight rooms
Locker rooms
Telecommunications
Other operating departments
Clubhouse
Administrative and general
Facility maintenance
Energy costs
    Total operating expenses   _____

INCOME BEFORE FIXED CHARGES   _____

FIXED CHARGES
Rent
Property taxes and other municipal charges
Insurance
Interest
Depreciation and amortization   _____
    Total fixed charges   _____

INCOME (LOSS) BEFORE TAXES   _____

PROVISION FOR INCOME TAXES   _____
    Results of operations   _____

OTHER ACTIVITIES
Initiation fees
Special assessments
Investment income
Other

INCREASE (DECREASE) IN UNRESTRICTED NET ASSETS (MEMBERS' EQUITY)

UNRESTRICTED NET ASSETS, BEGINNING OF PERIOD   _____

UNRESTRICTED NET ASSETS, END OF PERIOD $ _____

See notes to financial statements

Exhibit B-3

CITY OR COUNTRY CLUB
STATEMENT OF ACTIVITIES (FUND ACCOUNTING)
(External)

	Undesignated	Designated for Capital Replacements	Total
REVENUE			
Membership dues	$	$	$
Initiation fees			
Unused food minimums			
Food			
Beverage			
Entertainment			
Golf operations			
Golf shop			
Racquet sports			
Aquatic sports			
Other sports activities			
Overnight rooms			
Locker rooms			
Telecommunications			
Other operating departments			
Rentals and other revenue	_____	_____	_____
Total revenue	_____	_____	_____
OPERATING EXPENSES			
Food			
Beverage			
Entertainment			
Golf operations			
Golf shop			
Golf course maintenance			
Racquet operations			
Racquet shop			
Aquatic operations			
Other sports activities			
Overnight rooms			
Locker rooms			
Telecommunications			
Other operating departments			
Clubhouse			
Administrative and general			
Facility maintenance			
Energy costs	_____	_____	_____
Total operating expenses	_____	_____	_____
INCOME BEFORE FIXED CHARGES	_____	_____	_____
Rent			
Property taxes and other municipal charges			
Insurance			
Interest			
Depreciation and amortization	_____	_____	_____
Total fixed charges	_____	_____	_____
INCOME (LOSS) BEFORE TAXES	_____	_____	_____
PROVISION FOR INCOME TAXES	_____	_____	_____
Results of operations	_____	_____	_____
OTHER ACTIVITIES			
Initiation fees			
Special assessments			
Investment income			
Other			
INCREASE (DECREASE) IN UNRESTRICTED NET ASSETS (MEMBERS' EQUITY)			
UNRESTRICTED NET ASSETS, BEGINNING OF PERIOD			
UNRESTRICTED NET ASSETS, END OF PERIOD	$ _____	$ _____	$ _____

Note: please note that under the accounting literature, this method of reporting is optional.

STATEMENT OF CASH FLOWS

A complete financial presentation of a club should include a Statement of Cash Flows. One of the key purposes of the statement is to reflect fully the increase or decrease in cash and cash equivalents during the fiscal period. Professional accounting standards state that the Statement of Cash flows should reflect the operating, investing, and financing activities of an entity. Professional standards allow the Statement of Cash Flows to be prepared either on a direct or indirect basis. The example provided in Exhibit C is the indirect basis, which most clubs follow. This format can be used by both city and country clubs.

Exhibit C

STATEMENT OF CASH FLOWS
(Indirect Approach)

CASH FLOWS FROM OPERATING ACTIVITIES
  Increase (decrease) in unrestricted net assets $
  Adjustments to reconcile increase (decrease) in net assets to
    net cash provided (used) by operating activities
  Depreciation and amortization
  Deferred income taxes
  Revenue designated for capital replacements and improvements
  (Gains) losses on sales of investments
  (Increase) decrease in assets
    Accounts receivable
    Inventories
    Prepaid expenses
    Other current assets
    Security deposits
  Increase (decrease) in liabilities
    Accounts payable
    Taxes payable and accrued
    Accrued expenses
    Deferred revenue
    Special purpose funds
    Other current liabilities   ————
      Net cash provided (used) by operating activities ————

CASH FLOWS FROM INVESTING ACTIVITIES
  Deposits to designated assets
  Expenditures for property and equipment
  Purchases of investments
  Redemption of investments   ————
      Net cash provided (used) by investing activities ————

CASH FLOWS FROM FINANCING ACTIVITIES
  Revenue designated for capital replacement and improvements
  Proceeds of debt
  Repayment of debt
  Capital stock (membership certificates) sold
  Capital stock (membership certificates) redeemed ————
      Net cash provided (used) by financing activities ————

INCREASE (DECREASE) IN CASH AND CASH EQUIVALENTS ————

CASH AND CASH EQUIVALENTS, BEGINNING OF PERIOD ————

CASH AND CASH EQUIVALENTS, END OF PERIOD $ ————

SUPPLEMENTAL DISCLOSURE OF CASH FLOW INFORMATION:
  Interest paid during the year $
  Income taxes paid during the year $

See notes to financial statements.

NOTES TO FINANCIAL STATEMENTS

Explanatory notes are an essential ingredient for complete disclosure of the financial presentation of a club. Included in the notes should be a description of all significant accounting policies, as well as other items required for full disclosure. Commonly required disclosures would include policies relating to items such as inventory pricing method, method of valuing long-term assets, depreciation methods, recognition of income from dues, activity fees and initiation or entrance fees, designated special assessments and other significant assets, etc.

In addition, notes are necessary to provide full disclosure of all significant events or conditions reflected in the financial statements or as otherwise required by the rules of professional accounting. Items with respect to which all significant facts, if material, should be disclosed would include, but would not be limited to, the following:

- Brief description of the club (to include services to members and type of ownership)
- Retirement and/or deferred compensation plans
- Lease agreements
- Long-term debt agreements
- Contingent liabilities
- Pending lawsuits
- Income tax status
- Changes in accounting methods
- Extraordinary items of income or expense
- Long-term contracts
- Definition of cash and cash equivalents
- Description of designated assets
- Description of operating funds
- Use of significant estimates in preparing financial statements
- Long-term investment

Section 2
Statement of Activities—
Departmental Form

The Statement of Activities for clubs that presents information in departmental form follows the concept of responsibility accounting. Management usually prefers this form for internal use because it enables managers to monitor departmental performance and aids in decision–making situations.

The statements for city clubs and country clubs differ.

The Statement of Activities for city clubs (Exhibit D–1) starts with membership revenue. Both membership dues and initiation fees are shown; however, if the initiation fees are used for capital purposes, then they should be shown under other activities near the bottom of the statement. The next section of this statement includes clubhouse operating departments. Several are listed; however, any other areas of significant activity should be reported on a separate line. The summation of clubhouse operations is total clubhouse operating income (loss). The third section of a city club's Statement of Activities addresses undistributed operating expenses. This section includes administrative and general, clubhouse, facility maintenance, and energy costs. Clubhouse net (loss) is the clubhouse operating income (loss) minus the total undistributed operating expenses. Income before fixed charges is determined by adding clubhouse net to (or subtracting clubhouse loss from) total membership revenue. Income before fixed charges less fixed charges equals income (loss) before income taxes. Provision for income taxes, if any, is subtracted from income before income taxes to equal results of operations. The final section is other activities, which includes initiation fees not shown as membership revenue, special assessments, and investment income. Other activities that are significant should be separately reported. Insignificant other activities should be reported as other. The other activities are added to results of operations to equal increase in unrestricted net assets.

The Statement of Activities for country clubs (Exhibit D–2) differs in a few areas from the prescribed format for city clubs. The major differences relate to the sports activities. The second section of a country club's Statement of Activities addresses the cost of sports activities. It includes golf, racquet, aquatics, and any other significant sporting activities. The total of this section is net cost of sports activities. Total membership revenue less net cost of sports activities equals membership revenue available for clubhouse operations and fixed charges. Clubhouse operating income (loss) less undistributed operating expenses equals clubhouse operations and undistributed operating expense. Income before fixed charges is determined by subtracting clubhouse operations and undistributed operating expenses from membership revenue available for clubhouse operations and fixed charges. The remainder of the Statement of Activities for country clubs is very similar to that for city clubs as described above.

Any revenue or expense activity that is significant to the club will generally have a separate schedule. Otherwise, it will be consolidated with another department. Examples of expenses that may be included in administrative and general if insignificant, but otherwise have a separate schedule include:

- Front Office
- Board and Committee Charges
- Club Publications
- Membership (or Marketing) Department

Certain expenses are allocated from one department to several others. An example is the club's laundry. It is recommended that these allocations be made on a consistent and accurate basis.

Occasionally there may be significant extraordinary items of income or expense (such as gain or loss from the sale of property). Such items should be shown immediately preceding income taxes on the Statement of Activities.

The schedule references refer to the departmental schedules in Section 3.

Exhibit D-1

CITY CLUB
STATEMENT OF ACTIVITIES
(In Departmental Form)
(Internal)

	SCHEDULE	PERIOD ENDED	
MEMBERSHIP REVENUE			
Membership dues		$	$
Initiation fees			
Total membership revenue			
CLUBHOUSE OPERATING INCOME (LOSS)			
Food	A		
Beverage	B		
Entertainment	C		
Overnight rooms	D		
Health and fitness	K		
Telecommunications	M		
Other operating departments	N		
Rentals and other revenue	O		
Total clubhouse operating income (loss)			
UNDISTRIBUTED OPERATING EXPENSES			
Administrative and general	P		
Clubhouse	Q		
Facility maintenance	R		
Energy costs	R		
Total operating expenses			
Clubhouse net (loss)			
INCOME BEFORE FIXED CHARGES			
FIXED CHARGES	S		
Rent			
Property taxes and other municipal charges			
Insurance			
Interest			
Depreciation and amortization			
Total fixed charges			
INCOME (LOSS) BEFORE TAXES			
PROVISION FOR INCOME TAXES	S		
Results of operations			
OTHER ACTIVITIES			
Initiation fees			
Special assessments			
Investment income			
Other			
INCREASE (DECREASE) IN UNRESTRICTED NET ASSETS **(MEMBERS' EQUITY)**			
UNRESTRICTED NET ASSETS, BEGINNING OF PERIOD			
UNRESTRICTED NET ASSETS, END OF PERIOD		$	$

Exhibit D-2

COUNTRY CLUB
STATEMENT OF ACTIVITIES
(In Departmental Form)
(Internal)

	SCHEDULE	PERIOD ENDED	
MEMBERSHIP REVENUE			
Membership dues		$	$
Initiation fees			
Total membership revenue			
COST OF SPORTS ACTIVITIES			
Golf operations income (loss)	E		
Less golf course maintenance	G		
Golf shop	F		
Net golf profit (expense)			
Racquet sports	H		
Racquet shop	I		
Aquatic sports	J		
Other sports			
Net cost of sports activities			
Membership revenue available for clubhouse operations and fixed charges			
CLUBHOUSE OPERATING INCOME (LOSS)			
Food	A		
Beverage	B		
Entertainment	C		
Overnight rooms	D		
Locker rooms	L		
Telecommunications	M		
Other operating departments	N		
Rentals and other revenue	O		
Total clubhouse operating income (loss)			
UNDISTRIBUTED OPERATING EXPENSES			
Administrative and general	P		
Clubhouse	Q		
Facility maintenance	R		
Energy costs	R		
Total operating expenses			
Clubhouse operations and undistributed operating expenses			
INCOME BEFORE FIXED CHARGES			
FIXED CHARGES	S		
Rent			
Property taxes and other municipal charges			
Insurance			
Interest			
Depreciation and amortization			
Total fixed charges			
INCOME (LOSS) BEFORE TAXES			
PROVISION FOR INCOME TAXES	S		
Results of operations			
OTHER ACTIVITIES			
Initiation fees			
Special assessments			
Investment income			
Other			
INCREASE (DECREASE) IN UNRESTRICTED NET ASSETS (MEMBERS' EQUITY)			
UNRESTRICTED NET ASSETS, BEGINNING OF PERIOD			
UNRESTRICTED NET ASSETS, END OF PERIOD		$	$

Section 3
Departmental Schedules
(Selected Detail)

The operating schedules in this section support the financial presentation found in the Statement of Activities shown in Section II. These schedules detail revenue and expenses for the major revenue-producing departments, as well as overhead costs and expenses. The schedules provide detail concerning the operation of the club and are designed for management use. The main purpose of the section is to present financial data in a form that follows the concept of responsibility accounting. Each schedule essentially provides the appropriate committee chairman and/or department head with a Statement of Activities for the segment of the operation for which he or she is responsible. In addition, departmental operating schedules provide a basis for comparison with similar clubs and industry trends and enable club management to isolate and define the operating problems of each revenue and cost center.

Not all schedules or accounts will be appropriate for all clubs. Each club should select the schedules and accounts that meet its financial reporting needs.

City or Country Club
Food—Schedule A

FOOD SALES (LIST REVENUE BY LOCATION) $ _____

COST OF FOOD SOLD
   Cost of food consumed
   Less credit for employees' meals
   Less credit for gratis food   _____
      Cost of food sold   _____
         Gross profit on food sales   _____

OTHER REVENUE
   Unused minimum
   Dining room rental
      Total other revenue   _____
         Total gross profit and other revenue   _____

DEPARTMENTAL EXPENSES
   Payroll and related expenses
      Salaries and wages
      Less service charges
         Net salaries and wages   _____
      Payroll taxes and employee benefits
      Employees' meals   _____
         Total payroll and related expenses   _____
   Other expenses
      China, glassware, and silver
      Computer expense
      Contract services
      Dues and subscriptions
      Equipment rental
      Equipment repair and maintenance
      Gratis food
      Kitchen fuel
      Laundry and linen
      Licenses and permits
      Music and entertainment
      Operating supplies
      Printing and stationery
      Professional development
      Telephone
      Uniforms
      Other operating expenses
         Total other expenses   _____

TOTAL DEPARTMENTAL EXPENSES   _____

DEPARTMENTAL INCOME (LOSS) $ _____

Food—Schedule A illustrates a format and identifies line items that commonly appear on a supplemental schedule for food operations. This format and the line items will vary according to the needs and requirements of individual clubs. Therefore, the line items listed on the schedule may not apply to the food operation of every club. Individual clubs should modify the schedule to meet their own needs and requirements. Some clubs may even choose to combine food and beverage operations on a single supplemental schedule as shown in Appendix E.

Food Sales

Food Sales includes revenue derived from food sales, including sales of coffee, tea, milk, and soft drinks. The sales may be classified by outlet or the type of operation from which it is realized, such as dining room, lounge, banquets, and others. Sales should not include meals served to employees; the total of these, reduced to cost, should be deducted from the cost of food consumed and charged to the respective departments where the employees work. Allowances representing rebates and credits for overcharges on food sales should be charged directly against sales.

Cost of Food Sold

Cost of Food Consumed

Cost of Food Consumed includes the cost of food served to members, cost of food items furnished for employee meals, and the cost of gratis food. Clubs usually take a monthly food inventory. Cost of Food Consumed is calculated by adding total food purchases to the value of the inventory at the beginning of the month and then subtracting the value of the inventory at the end of the month. Total food purchases are calculated by subtracting trade discounts (but not cash discounts) from the gross invoice price for all food items and then adding charges for transportation, delivery, and storage. If the policy of the club permits commissary and steward's sales, they should be credited to cost of food sales when they are sold, at cost or a nominal mark-up. When the income on such sales is of sufficient importance to warrant it, the amount should be included in Food Sales, and the cost of such sales charged to Cost of Food Consumed.

Employees' Meals

Clubs should calculate the cost of employees' meals either by an exact cost system, or, in cases where such a system is unwarranted, by a fixed price per meal. Regardless of the method used, the cost of furnishing meals for employees of the various departments within the property should be charged to those departments. These charges appear as an expense on appropriate departmental schedules under Employees' Meals.

Gratis Food

Clubs should calculate the cost of gratis food provided to members and others (not employees) and the amounts should be charged to those departments serving the gratis food. These charges appear as an expense on appropriate departmental schedules under Gratis Food.

Cost of Food Sold

Cost of Food Sold is calculated by subtracting the Cost of Employee Meals and Gratis Food from Cost of Food Consumed.

Gross Profit on Food Sales

Gross Profit on Food Sales is determined by subtracting Cost of Food Sold from Food Sales.

Other Revenue

Other Revenue includes revenue from sources other than the sale of food, including unused food minimums and dining room rentals.

Unused Minimum

These charges should be reflected in this category because of their direct relationship to the food operation. Many clubs treat these charges as Other Revenue to avoid a distortion in food gross profits.

Dining Room Rental

Revenue derived from the rental of private and dining and meeting rooms that are used in connection with the service of food should be included in this item.

Total Other Revenue

Total Other Revenue is calculated by adding all of the amounts listed under Other Revenue.

Total Gross Profit and Other Revenue

This amount is calculated by adding Gross Profit on Food Sales and Total Other Revenue.

Departmental Expenses

Salaries and Wages

Salaries and Wages includes regular pay, overtime pay, vacation pay, sick pay, holiday pay, incentive pay, severance pay, distributed service charges, and bonuses for employees of the food department. This line item should also include any expense associated with leased labor, but not contract labor, which should be charged to Contract Services or the relevant expense line item. If leased labor expense is significant, a separate line item called Leased Labor should be created and listed immediately after Salaries and Wages.

Service Charges

Service charges not distributed to employees should be subtracted from salaries and wages. Many clubs in the club industry have automatically charged their members a set percentage of the members' purchases of food and beverages. This involuntary charge is generally referred to simply as a service charge. The use of service charges varies across the many clubs constituting the club industry. Often, clubs use a service charge effectively to offset part of their labor costs. When the club pays the entire service charge to its employees, the proper labor costs should be reduced by the amount of the service charge to the members. If the club retains a major portion of the service charge, the portion of the service charge levied to raise revenues should be credited to Other Revenue and the portion meant to offset labor costs should be credited to the proper labor cost accounts. The major reason for the labor offset is for comparison purposes between a club that tips versus a club that uses a service charge. Gratuities (also referred to as tips by some clubs) are voluntary on the part of the members. Since these amounts are paid to the employees, they should be credited to the proper labor cost accounts.

Payroll Taxes and Employee Benefits

Payroll Taxes and Employee Benefits includes payroll taxes, payroll-related insurance expense, retirement, and other payroll-related expenses applicable to the food department.

Employees' Meals

The cost of meals furnished to employees whose salaries and wages are charged to the food department is included in this item.

Total Payroll and Related Expenses

Total Payroll and Related Expenses is calculated by adding Net Salaries and Wages to Payroll Taxes and Employee Benefits and Employees' Meals.

Other Expenses

This expense grouping includes significant food department expenses. Items appearing under Other Expenses vary from club to club. Examples of items that commonly appear as Other Expenses follow.

China, Glassware, and Silver. This item includes the cost of the china, glassware, and silver used in providing food service to the clubs' members. These expenses are usually accounted for in separate general ledger accounts.

Computer Expense. This item includes all expenses related to computer usage, including repairs and service contracts, supplies, and minor replacements. Major replacements should be capitalized and depreciated.

Contract Services. Contract Services includes any expenses associated with an activity that is normally charged to the department, but is now outsourced. Examples include the cost of contracting outside companies to wash windows, degrease hoods, clean carpets and rugs, and exterminate and disinfect areas of the food department. Contract Services also includes the cost of maintaining the point-of-sale system and equipment.

Dues and Subscriptions. This account should be charged with the cost of memberships, subscriptions to newspapers and magazines, and books used by employees in the food department.

Equipment Rental. The cost of equipment rented for use in the food department should be charged to this account.

Equipment Repair and Maintenance. This account is charged with the cost of materials used in maintaining and repairing items in the food department. The cost of work performed by outside contractors is also charged to this account.

Gratis Food. The cost of gratis food, including bottled water, provided to members and guests (not employees) interacting with the food department is charged to this account.

Kitchen Fuel. This account should be charged with cost of fuel used for cooking.

Laundry and Linen. This account should include both the laundry costs assigned to this department and the cost of linen and/or rental linen services used by the food department.

Licenses and Permits. Licenses and Permits includes the costs of all federal, state, and municipal licenses and permits for the food facilities of the property.

Music and Entertainment. This item includes all the costs associated with providing entertainment within the club's food facilities.

Operating Supplies. Operating Supplies includes the cost of cleaning supplies, menus, paper supplies (other than stationery), utensils, and similar operating expenses applicable to the food department. If the cost of any of these items is significant, items and amounts should be listed separately from Operating Supplies.

- *Cleaning Supplies.* This item includes the costs associated with keeping food areas and equipment clean and sanitary.

- *Menus.* This item includes the cost associated with producing menus, such as the cost of artwork, printing, and menu covers.

- *Paper Supplies.* This item includes the costs of paper supplies (other than stationery) used by the food department.

- *Utensils.* This item includes the cost of all tools needed in the process of food preparation, such as butcher knives, spatulas, and whisks.

Printing and Stationery. The cost of printed forms, service manuals, stationery, and office supplies that are purchased from outside printers or produced internally should be charged to this account when they are used by employees of the food department.

Professional Development. Professional development includes costs other than time associated with training employees. Examples include the costs of training materials, supplies, instructor fees, and outside seminars and conferences.

Telephone. Any telephone expenditures that can be directly related to the food department should be charged to this account.

Uniforms. This item includes the cost or rental of uniforms for employees of the food department, as well as the cost of repairing uniforms of food department employees.

Other Operating Expenses. This item includes costs of operating expenses applicable to the food department that do not apply to other line items discussed for this department.

Total Other Expenses

Total Other Expenses is calculated by adding all items listed under Other Expenses.

Total Departmental Expenses

Total Departmental Expenses is calculated by adding Total Payroll and Related Expenses to Total Other Expenses.

Departmental Income (Loss)

The income (or loss) of the food department is calculated by subtracting Total Departmental Expenses from Total Gross Profit and Other Revenue.

City or Country Club
Beverage—Schedule B

BEVERAGE SALES (LIST REVENUE BY LOCATION)	$ _____
COST OF BEVERAGE SOLD	_____
Gross profit on beverage sales	_____
OTHER REVENUE	_____
Total gross profit and other revenue	_____
DEPARTMENTAL EXPENSES	
Payroll and related expenses	
Salaries and wages	
Less service charges	_____
Net salaries and wages	_____
Payroll taxes and employee benefits	
Employees' meals	_____
Total payroll and related expenses	_____
Other expenses	
China, glassware, and silver	
Computer expense	
Contract services	
Dues and subscriptions	
Equipment rental	
Equipment repair and maintenance	
Gratis food	
Laundry and linen	
Licenses and permits	
Music and entertainment	
Operating supplies	
Printing and stationery	
Professional development	
Telephone	
Uniforms	
Other operating expenses	_____
Total other expenses	_____
TOTAL DEPARTMENTAL EXPENSES	_____
DEPARTMENTAL INCOME (LOSS)	$ _____

Beverage—Schedule B illustrates a format and identifies line items that commonly appear on a supplemental schedule for beverage operations. This format and the line items will vary according to the needs and requirements of individual clubs. Therefore, the line items listed on the schedule may not apply to the beverage operation of every club. Individual clubs should modify this schedule accordingly. Some clubs may even choose to combine food and beverage operations on a single supplementary schedule as shown in Appendix E.

Beverage Sales

Beverage Sales should be credited with revenue derived from beverage sales. The sales may be classified by bars, dining rooms, room service, parties, and banquets;

sales may also be segregated into wines, liquors, and beers. Corkage charges should not be reflected in beverage sales, but should be credited to Other Revenue in the beverage department. Credits for overcharges on beverage sales should be charged directly against sales. If sales or gross receipt taxes are charged to clubs, they should be deducted from sales and not shown as expense.

Cost of Beverage Sold

Cost of Beverage Sold represents the cost of liquors, wines, beers, mineral waters, and mixes used in the preparation of drinks served to members and guests at gross invoice price less trade discounts (but not cash discounts), plus import duties, transportation, delivery, storage, and taxes. Cost of Beverage Sold is calculated by adding total beverage purchases to the value of the inventory at the beginning of the month and then subtracting the value of the inventory at the end of the month. To this cost is added the cost of food items such as eggs, syrups, sugar, fruits, and soft drinks used in the preparation of mixed drinks. Beverage Sales should be charged with the cost of barrels, bottles, or other containers and credited with deposit refunds and sales thereof.

Gross Profit on Beverage Sales

Gross Profit on Beverage Sales is determined by subtracting the Cost of Beverage Sold from Beverage Sales.

Other Revenue

Beverage revenue from sources other than the actual sale of beverage should be included in this caption.

Total Gross Profit and Other Revenue

This amount is determined by summing Gross Profit on Beverage Sales and Other Revenue.

Departmental Expenses

Salaries and Wages

Salaries and Wages includes regular pay, overtime pay, vacation pay, sick pay, holiday pay, incentive pay, severance pay, distributed service charges, and bonuses for employees of the beverage department. This line item should also include any expense associated with leased labor, but not contract labor, which should be charged to Contract Services or the relevant expense line item. If leased labor expense is significant, a separate line item called Leased Labor should be created and listed immediately after Salaries and Wages.

Service Charges

Service charges not distributed to employees should be subtracted from salaries and wages. Many clubs in the club industry have automatically charged their members a set percentage of the members' purchases of food and beverages. This involuntary charge is generally referred to simply as a service charge. The use of service charges varies across the many clubs constituting the club industry. Often, clubs use a service charge effectively to offset part of their labor costs. When the club pays the entire service charge to its employees, the proper labor costs should be reduced by the amount of the service charge to the members. If the club retains a major portion of the service charge, the portion of the service charge levied to raise revenues should be credited to Other Revenue and the portion meant to offset labor costs should be credited to the proper labor cost accounts. The major reason for the labor offset is for comparison purposes between a club that tips versus a club that uses a service charge. Gratuities (also referred to as tips by some clubs) are voluntary on the part of the members. Since these amounts are paid to the employees, they should be credited to the proper labor cost accounts.

Payroll Taxes and Employee Benefits

Payroll Taxes and Employee Benefits includes payroll taxes, payroll-related insurance expense, retirement, and other payroll-related expenses applicable to the beverage department.

Employees' Meals

The cost of meals furnished to employees whose salaries and wages are charged to the beverage department is included in this item.

Total Payroll and Related Expenses

Total Payroll and Related Expenses is calculated by adding Net Salaries and Wages to Payroll Taxes and Employee Benefits and Employees' Meals.

Other Expenses

This expense grouping includes significant beverage department expenses. Items appearing under Other Expenses vary from club to club. Examples of items that commonly appear as Other Expenses follow:

China, Glassware, and Silver. This item includes the cost of the china, glassware, and silver used in providing beverage service to the clubs' members and guests. These expenses are usually accounted for in separate general ledger accounts.

Computer Expense. This item includes all expenses related to computer usage, including repairs and service contracts, supplies, and minor replacements. Major replacements should be capitalized and depreciated.

Contract Services. Contract Services includes any expenses associated with an activity that is normally charged to the department, but is now outsourced. Examples include the cost of contracting outside companies to wash windows, clean carpets and rugs, and exterminate and disinfect areas of the beverage department. Contract Services also includes the cost of maintaining the point-of-sale system and equipment of this department.

Dues and Subscriptions. This account should be charged with the cost of memberships, subscriptions to newspapers and magazines, and books used by employees in the beverage department.

Equipment Rental. The cost of equipment rented for use in the beverage department should be charged to this account.

Equipment Repair and Maintenance. This account is charged with the cost of materials used in maintaining and repairing items in the beverage department. The cost of work performed by outside contractors is also charged to this account.

Gratis Food. The cost of gratis food, including bottled water, provided to members and guests (not employees) interacting with the beverage department is charged to this account.

Laundry and Linen. This account should include both the laundry costs assigned to this department and the cost of linen and/or rental linen services used by the beverage department.

Licenses and Permits. Licenses and Permits includes the costs of all federal, state, and municipal licenses and permits for the beverage facilities of the property, including liquor licenses.

Music and Entertainment. This item includes all the costs associated with providing entertainment within the club's beverage facilities.

Operating Supplies. Operating Supplies includes the cost of cleaning supplies, beverage lists, paper supplies (other than stationery), utensils, and similar operating expenses applicable to the beverage department. If the cost of any of these items is significant, items and amounts should be listed separately from Operating Supplies.

- *Cleaning Supplies.* This item includes the costs associated with keeping beverage areas and equipment clean and sanitary.

- *Beverage Lists.* This item includes the cost associated with producing wine and drink menus, such as the cost of artwork, printing, and menu covers.

- *Paper Supplies.* This item includes the costs of paper supplies used by the beverage department.

- *Utensils.* This item includes the cost of all tools needed in the beverage department.

Printing and Stationery. This cost of printed forms, service manuals, stationery, and office supplies that are purchased from outside printers or produced internally should be charged to this account when they are used by employees of the beverage department.

Professional Development. Professional development includes costs other than time associated with training beverage employees. Examples include the costs of training materials, supplies, instructor fees, and outside seminars and conferences.

Telephone. Any telephone expenditures that can be directly related to the beverage department should be charged to this account.

Uniforms. This item includes the cost or rental of uniforms for employees of the beverage department, as well as the cost of repairing uniforms of beverage department employees.

Other Operating Expenses. This item includes costs of operating expenses applicable to the beverage department that do not apply to other line items discussed for this department.

Total Other Expenses

Total Other Expenses is calculated by adding all items listed under Other Expenses.

Total Departmental Expenses

Total Departmental Expenses is calculated by adding Total Payroll and Related Expenses to Total Other Expenses.

Departmental Income (Loss)

The income (or loss) of the beverage department is calculated by subtracting Total Departmental Expenses from the amount shown as Total Gross Profit and Other Revenue.

City or Country Club
Entertainment—Schedule C

REVENUE $ _____

DEPARTMENTAL EXPENSES
   Payroll and related expenses
      Salaries and wages
      Payroll taxes and employee benefits
      Employees' meals   _____
         Total payroll and related expenses   _____
   Other expenses
      Committee expenses
      Computer expense
      Contract entertainment
      Contract services
      Decorations and props
      Dues and subscriptions
      Equipment rental
      Equipment repair and maintenance
      Films
      Gratis food
      Laundry and linen
      Licenses and permits
      Operating supplies
      Printing and stationery
      Prizes
      Professional development
      Royalties
      Telephone
      Uniforms
      Other operating expenses   _____
         Total other expenses   _____

TOTAL DEPARTMENTAL EXPENSES   _____

DEPARTMENTAL INCOME (LOSS) $ _____

Entertainment—Schedule C illustrates a format and identifies line items that commonly appear on a supplemental schedule for entertainment. This format and the line items will vary according to the needs and requirements of individual clubs. Therefore, the line items listed on the schedule may not apply to the entertainment department of every club. Individual clubs should modify the schedule to meet their own needs and requirements.

Revenue

Any revenue derived from the sale of tickets, admissions, charges, etc., designed to cover the cost of special parties and club-wide entertainment events should be credited to this account.

Departmental Expenses

Salaries and Wages

Salaries and Wages includes regular pay, overtime pay, vacation pay, sick pay, holiday pay, incentive pay, severance pay, and bonuses for employees of the entertainment department. This line item should also include any expense associated with leased labor, but not contract labor, which should be charged to Contract Services, Contract Entertainment, or the relevant expense line item. If leased labor expense is significant, a separate line item called Leased Labor should be created and listed immediately after Salaries and Wages.

Payroll Taxes and Employee Benefits

Payroll Taxes and Employee Benefits includes payroll taxes, payroll-related insurance expense, retirement, and other payroll-related expenses applicable to the entertainment department.

Employees' Meals

The cost of meals furnished to employees whose salaries and wages are charged to the entertainment department is included in this expense item.

Total Payroll and Related Expenses

Total Payroll and Related Expenses is calculated by adding Salaries and Wages to Payroll Taxes and Employee Benefits and Employees' Meals.

Other Expenses

This expense grouping includes significant entertainment department expenses. Items appearing under Other Expenses vary from club to club. Examples of items that commonly appear as Other Expenses follow.

Committee Expenses. This account includes the committee expenses, including printing and postage, related to club events such as concerts (not including dining room music), lectures, movies, travelogues, open houses, special member parties, etc.

Computer Expense. This item includes all expenses related to computer usage, including repairs and service contracts, supplies, and minor replacements. Major replacements should be capitalized and depreciated.

Contract Entertainment. This account is charged with the cost of entertainers' and musicians' contracts and includes transportation, gifts to entertainers, etc.

Contract Services. Contract Services includes any expenses associated with an activity that is normally charged to the department, but is now outsourced. Examples include the cost of contracting outside companies to plan and execute special and/or club-wide entertainment events.

Decorations and Props. This account includes the cost of decorations and props.

Dues and Subscriptions. This account should be charged with the cost of memberships, subscriptions to newspapers and magazines, and books used by employees in the entertainment department.

Equipment Rental. The cost of equipment rented for use in the entertainment department should be charged to this account.

Equipment Repair and Maintenance. This account is charged with the cost of materials used in maintaining and repairing items in the entertainment department. The cost of work performed by outside contractors is also charged to this account.

Films. This account is charged with the cost of film rental and outside projectionist salaries.

Gratis Food. The cost of gratis food, including bottled water, provided to entertainers as well as members and guests (not employees) interacting with the entertainers and entertainment department is charged to this account.

Laundry and Linen. This account should include both the laundry costs assigned to this department and the cost of linen and/or rental linen services used by the entertainment department.

Licenses and Permits. Licenses and Permits includes the costs of all licenses and permits required for club-wide entertainment events excluding those pertaining to royalties.

Operating Supplies. Operating Supplies includes the cost of cleaning supplies, paper supplies (other than stationery), and similar operating expenses applicable to the entertainment department. If the cost of any of these items is significant, items and amounts should be listed separately from Operating Supplies.

Printing and Stationery. This cost of printed forms, service manuals, stationery, and office supplies that are purchased from outside printers or produced internally should be charged to this account when they are used by employees of the entertainment department.

Prizes. This item includes the cost of prizes purchased for entertainment functions.

Professional Development. Professional development includes costs other than time associated with training entertainment department employees. Examples include the costs of training materials, supplies, instructor fees, and outside seminars and conferences.

Royalties. This includes licensing fees paid to ASCAP, BMI, SESAC, MPLC, and other similar organizations.

Telephone. Any telephone expenditures that can be directly related to the entertainment department should be charged to this account.

Uniforms. This item includes the cost or rental of uniforms for employees of the entertainment department, as well as the cost of repairing uniforms of entertainment department employees.

Other Operating Expenses. This item includes costs of operating expenses applicable to the entertainment department that do not apply to other line items discussed for this department.

Total Other Expenses

Total Other Expenses is calculated by adding all items listed under Other Expenses.

Total Departmental Expenses

Total Departmental Expenses is calculated by adding Total Payroll and Related Expenses to Total Other Expenses.

Departmental Income (Loss)

The income (or loss) of the entertainment department is calculated by subtracting Total Departmental Expenses from Revenue.

City or Country Club
Overnight Rooms—Schedule D

REVENUE
  Transient $
  Permanent
  Other   ——————
    Total revenue   ——————

DEPARTMENTAL EXPENSES
  Payroll and related expenses
    Salaries and wages
    Payroll taxes and employee benefits
    Employees' meals   ——————
      Total payroll and related expenses ——————
  Other expenses
    Cable/satellite television
    China, glassware, and silver
    Computer expense
    Contract services
    Dues and subscriptions
    Equipment rental
    Equipment repairs and maintenance
    Gratis food
    Laundry and linen
    Member and guest supplies
    Operating supplies
    Printing and stationery
    Professional development
    Telephone
    Uniforms
    Other operating expenses   ——————
      Total other expenses   ——————

TOTAL DEPARTMENTAL EXPENSES   ——————

DEPARTMENTAL INCOME (LOSS) $ ══════

Overnight Rooms—Schedule D illustrates a format and identifies line items that commonly appear on a supplemental schedule for overnight rooms operations. This format and the line items will vary according to the needs and requirements of individual clubs. Therefore, the line items listed on the schedule may not apply to the overnight rooms operations of every club. Individual clubs should modify the schedule to meet their own needs and requirements.

Revenue

Transient/Permanent

All revenue derived from sleeping rooms should be reflected in this section, segregated into revenue from permanent member residents and that from transient guests and members. Rooms revenue should be classified as permanent only when the member or guest has established a residence in the club for an extended period. Any allowances should be netted against revenue.

Other

Other revenue includes overnight rooms revenue other than that recorded in transient and permanent. An example would be movie rentals.

Departmental Expenses

Salaries and Wages

Salaries and Wages includes regular pay, overtime pay, vacation pay, sick pay, holiday pay, incentive pay, severance pay, and bonuses for employees of the overnight rooms department. This line item should also include any expense associated with leased labor, but not contract labor, which should be charged to Contract Services or the relevant expense line item. If leased labor expense is significant, a separate line item called Leased Labor should be created and listed immediately after Salaries and Wages.

Payroll Taxes and Employee Benefits

Payroll Taxes and Employee Benefits includes payroll taxes, payroll-related insurance expense, retirement, and other payroll-related expenses applicable to the overnight rooms department.

Employees' Meals

The cost of meals furnished to employees whose salaries and wages are charged to the overnight rooms department is included in this expense item.

Total Payroll and Related Expenses

Total Payroll and Related Expenses is calculated by adding Salaries and Wages to Payroll Taxes and Employee Benefits and Employees' Meals.

Other Expenses

This expense grouping includes significant overnight rooms department expenses. Items appearing under Other Expenses vary from club to club. Examples of items that commonly appear as Other Expenses follow.

Cable/Satellite Television. The cost of cable/satellite television for the overnight rooms department should be recorded in this account.

China, Glassware, and Silver. This item includes the cost of the china, glassware, and silver provided in overnight rooms for the use of the clubs' members and guests. These expenses are usually accounted for in separate general ledger accounts.

Computer Expense. This item includes all expenses related to computer usage, including repairs and service contracts, supplies, and minor replacements. Major replacements should be capitalized and depreciated.

Contract Services. Contract Services includes any expenses associated with an activity that is normally charged to the department, but is now outsourced. Examples include the cost of contracting outside companies to wash windows, clean carpets and rugs, and exterminate and disinfect areas of the overnight rooms department.

Dues and Subscriptions. This account should be charged with the cost of memberships, subscriptions to newspapers and magazines, and books used by employees in the overnight rooms department.

Equipment Rental. The cost of equipment rented for use in the overnight rooms department should be charged to this account.

Equipment Repair and Maintenance. This account is charged with the cost of materials used in maintaining and repairing items in the overnight rooms department. The cost of work performed by outside contractors is also charged to this account.

Gratis Food. The cost of gratis food, including bottled water, provided to members and others (not employees) interacting with the overnight rooms department is charged to this account.

Laundry and Linen. This account should include both the laundry costs assigned to this department and the cost of towels, linen, and/or rental linen services used by the overnight rooms department.

Member and Guest Supplies. This item includes the cost of overnight rooms supplies and amenities that are provided gratis to overnight members and guests.

Operating Supplies. Operating Supplies includes the cost of cleaning supplies, paper supplies (other than stationery), and similar operating expenses applicable to the overnight rooms department. If the cost of any of these items is significant, items and amounts should be listed separately from Operating Supplies.

Printing and Stationery. This cost of printed forms, service manuals, stationery, and office supplies that are purchased from outside printers or produced internally should be charged to this account when they are used by employees of the overnight rooms department.

Professional Development. Professional development includes costs other than time associated with training employees. Examples include the costs of training materials, supplies, instructor fees, and outside seminars and conferences.

Telephone. Any telephone expenditures that can be directly related to the overnight rooms department should be charged to this account.

Uniforms. This item includes the cost or rental of uniforms for employees of the overnight rooms department, as well as the cost of repairing uniforms of overnight rooms department employees.

Other Operating Expenses. This item includes costs of operating expenses applicable to the overnight rooms department that do not apply to other line items discussed for this department.

Total Other Expenses

Total Other Expenses is calculated by adding all items listed under Other Expenses

Total Departmental Expenses

Total Departmental Expenses is calculated by adding Total Payroll and Related Expenses to Total Other Expenses.

Departmental Income (Loss)

The income (or loss) of the overnight rooms department is calculated by subtracting Total Departmental Expenses from Total Revenue.

Country Club
Golf Operations—Schedule E

REVENUE
   Greens fees $
   Guest fees
   Trail fees
   Club storage
   Club rentals
   Club repair
   Range fees
   Tournament fees
   Cart rentals
   Service of member-owned carts
   Lessons
   Other   _____
      Total revenue   _____

DEPARTMENTAL EXPENSES
   Payroll and related expenses
      Salaries and wages
      Payroll taxes and employee benefits
      Employees' meals   _____
         Total payroll and related expenses   _____
   Other expenses
      Cart rentals
      Computer expense
      Contract professionals
      Driving range
      Dues and subscriptions
      Electricity
      Equipment rental
      Equipment repair and maintenance
      Gasoline and lubricants
      Golf cart batteries
      Golf cart repairs and maintenance
      Gratis food
      Laundry and linen
      Operating supplies
      Printing and stationery
      Prizes
      Professional development
      Telephone
      Tournament expenses
      Uniforms
      Vehicle expense
      Other operating expenses   _____
      Total other expenses   _____

TOTAL DEPARTMENTAL EXPENSES   _____

DEPARTMENTAL INCOME (LOSS) $ _____

Golf Operations—Schedule E illustrates a format and identifies line items that commonly appear on a supplemental schedule for golf operations. This format and the line items will vary according to the needs and requirements of individual clubs. Therefore, the line items listed on the schedule may not apply to golf operations of every club. Individual clubs should modify the schedule to meet their own needs and requirements. *Note:* When tournament activities are significant, a club may desire to show a separate schedule reflecting tournament revenues and expenses.

Revenue

Golf operations revenue includes greens fees, guest fees, trail fees, club storage, club rentals, club repair, range fees, tournament fees, cart rentals, service of member-owned carts, lessons, and other.

Departmental Expenses

Salaries and Wages

Salaries and Wages includes regular pay, overtime pay, vacation pay, sick pay, holiday pay, incentive pay, lessons and clinics pay, severance pay, and bonuses for employees of the golf operations department. This line item should also include any expense associated with leased labor, but not contract labor, which should be charged to Contract Professionals or the relevant expense line item. If leased labor expense is significant, a separate line item called Leased Labor should be created and listed immediately after Salaries and Wages.

Payroll Taxes and Employee Benefits

Payroll Taxes and Employee Benefits includes payroll taxes, payroll-related insurance expense, retirement, and other payroll-related expenses applicable to the golf operations department.

Employees' Meals

The cost of meals furnished to employees whose salaries and wages are charged to the golf operations department is included in this expense item.

Total Payroll and Related Expenses

Total Payroll and Related Expenses is calculated by adding Salaries and Wages to Payroll Taxes and Employee Benefits and Employees' Meals.

Other Expenses

This expense grouping includes significant golf operations department expenses. Items appearing under Other Expenses vary from club to club. Examples of items that commonly appear as Other Expenses follow:

Cart Rentals. This account should be charges for the cost of cart rentals.

Computer Expense. This item includes all expenses related to computer usage, including repairs and service contracts, supplies, and minor replacements. Major replacements should be capitalized and depreciated.

Contract Professionals. Amounts paid to golf professionals under contract and not on the payroll should be charged to this account.

Driving Range. The costs associated with the driving range, such as markers, golf balls, and pails, should be recorded in this account.

Dues and Subscriptions. This account should be charged with the cost of memberships, subscriptions to newspapers and magazines, and books used by employees in the golf operations department.

Electricity. The cost of electricity to charge golf cart batteries and for other golf operations purposes should be charged to this account.

Equipment Rental. The cost of equipment rented for use in the golf operations, other than cart rentals, should be charged to this account.

Equipment Repair and Maintenance. This account is charged with the cost of materials used in maintaining and repairing equipment, other than golf carts, in the golf operations department. The cost of repairing golf carts should be shown as Golf Cart Repairs and Maintenance. The cost of work performed by outside contractors is also charged to this account.

Gasoline and Lubricants. The cost of gasoline and lubricants for gas powered golf carts is charged to this account.

Golf Cart Batteries. The cost of batteries should be charged to this account. If capitalized, the batteries would be shown as equipment on the Statement of Financial Position and depreciated.

Golf Cart Repairs and Maintenance. The cost of repairs and maintenance of golf carts should be charged to this account.

Gratis Food. The cost of gratis food, including bottled water, provided to members and guests (not employees) interacting with the golf operations department is charged to this account.

Laundry and Linen. This account should include the laundry costs assigned to this department.

Operating Supplies. Operating Supplies includes the cost of cleaning supplies, paper supplies (other than stationery), and similar operating expenses applicable to the golf operations department. If the cost of any of these items is significant, items and amounts should be listed separately from Operating Supplies.

Printing and Stationery. This cost of printed forms, service manuals, stationery, and office supplies that are purchased from outside printers or produced internally should be charged to this account when they are used by employees of the golf operations department.

Prizes. The cost of prizes awarded by the golf operations department should be recorded in this account.

Professional Development. Professional development includes costs other than time associated with training golf operations employees. Examples include the costs of training materials, supplies, instructor fees, and outside seminars and conferences.

Telephone. Any telephone expenditures that can be directly related to the golf operations department should be charged to this account.

Tournament Expenses. All expenses incurred in administering golf tournaments should be charged to this account. *Note:* When tournament activities are significant, a club may desire to show a separate schedule reflecting tournament revenues and expenses.

Uniforms. This item includes the cost or rental of uniforms for employees of the golf operations department, as well as the cost of repairing uniforms of golf operations department employees.

Vehicle Expense. The costs of operating and/or renting vehicles used by this department are recorded in this account.

Other Operating Expenses. This item includes costs of operating expenses applicable to the golf operations department that do not apply to other line items discussed for this department.

Total Other Expenses

Total Other Expenses is calculated by adding all items listed under Other Expenses.

Total Departmental Expenses

Total Departmental Expenses is calculated by adding Total Payroll and Related Expenses to Total Other Expenses.

Departmental Income (Loss)

The income (loss) of the golf operations department is calculated by subtracting Total Departmental Expenses from Total Revenue.

Country Club
Golf Shop—Schedule F

REVENUE	$ _____
COST OF MERCHANDISE SOLD	_____
Gross profit on golf shop revenue	_____
DEPARTMENTAL EXPENSES	
Payroll and related expenses	
Salaries and wages	
Payroll taxes and employee benefits	
Employees' meals	_____
Total payroll and related expenses	_____
Other expenses	
Computer expense	
Contract services	
Dues and subscriptions	
Equipment rental	
Equipment repair and maintenance	
Gratis food	
Laundry and linen	
Operating supplies	
Printing and stationery	
Professional development	
Telephone	
Uniforms	
Other operating expenses	_____
Total other expenses	_____
TOTAL DEPARTMENTAL EXPENSES	_____
DEPARTMENTAL INCOME (LOSS)	$ _____

Golf Shop—Schedule F illustrates a format and identifies line items that commonly appear on a supplemental schedule for a club's golf shop when the club owns the shop. This format and the line items will vary according to the needs and requirements of individual clubs. Therefore, the line items listed on the schedule may not apply to golf shop of every club. Individual clubs should modify the schedule to meet their own needs and requirements.

Revenue

Revenue is credited for sales of merchandise in the golf shop. Allowances representing rebated and credits on golf shop revenue should be charged directly against revenue.

Cost of Merchandise Sold

Cost of Merchandise Sold represents the purchase price of merchandise sold in the golf shop, less trade discounts (but not cash discounts), plus transportation, storage, and delivery charges. The amount may be derived by taking the value of inventory at the beginning of the period, adding total purchases, and subtracting ending inventory.

Gross Profit on Golf Shop Revenue

This is determined by subtracting Cost of Merchandise Sold from Revenue.

Departmental Expenses

Salaries and Wages

Salaries and Wages includes regular pay, overtime pay, vacation pay, sick pay, holiday pay, incentive pay, severance pay, and bonuses for employees of the golf shop. This line item should also include any expense associated with leased labor, but not contract labor, which should be charged to Contract Services or the relevant expense line item. If leased labor expense is significant, a separate line item called Leased Labor should be created and listed immediately after Salaries and Wages.

Payroll Taxes and Employee Benefits

Payroll Taxes and Employee Benefits includes payroll taxes, payroll-related insurance expense, retirement, and other payroll-related expenses applicable to the golf shop.

Employees' Meals

The cost of meals furnished to employees whose salaries and wages are charged to the golf shop is included in this expense item.

Total Payroll and Related Expenses

Total Payroll and Related Expenses is calculated by adding Salaries and Wages to Payroll Taxes and Employee Benefits and Employees' Meals.

Other Expenses

This expense grouping includes significant golf shop expenses. Items appearing under Other Expenses vary from club to club. Examples of items that commonly appear as Other Expenses follow:

Computer Expense. This item includes all expenses related to computer usage, including repairs and service contracts, supplies, and minor replacements. Major replacements should be capitalized and depreciated.

Contract Services. Contract Services includes any expenses associated with an activity that is normally charged to the department, but is now outsourced. Examples include the cost of contracting outside companies to wash windows and clean carpets and rugs in the golf shop.

Dues and Subscriptions. This account should be charged with the cost of memberships, subscriptions to newspapers and magazines, and books used by employees in the golf shop.

Equipment Rental. The cost of equipment rented for use in the golf shop should be charged to this account.

Equipment Repair and Maintenance. This account is charged with the cost of materials used in maintaining and repairing equipment in the golf shop. The cost of work performed by outside contractors is also charged to this account.

Gratis Food. The cost of gratis food, including bottled water, provided to members and guests (not employees) interacting with the golf shop is charged to this account.

Laundry and Linen. This account should include the laundry costs assigned to this department.

Operating Supplies. Operating Supplies includes the cost of cleaning supplies, paper supplies (other than stationery), and similar operating expenses applicable to the golf shop. If the cost of any of these items is significant, items and amounts should be listed separately from Operating Supplies.

Printing and Stationery. This cost of printed forms, service manuals, stationery, and office supplies that are purchased from outside printers or produced internally should be charged to this account when they are used by employees of the golf shop.

Professional Development. Professional development includes cost other than time associated with training golf shop employees. Examples include the costs of training materials, supplies, instructor fees, and outside seminars and conferences.

Telephone. Any telephone expenditures that can be directly related to the golf shop should be charged to this account.

Uniforms. This item includes the cost or rental of uniforms for employees of the golf shop, as well as the cost of repairing uniforms of golf shop employees.

Other Operating Expenses. This item includes costs of operating expenses applicable to the golf shop that do not apply to other line items discussed for this department.

Total Other Expenses

Total Other Expenses is calculated by adding all items listed under Other Expenses.

Total Departmental Expenses

Total Departmental Expenses is calculated by adding Total Payroll and Related Expenses to Total Other Expenses.

Departmental Income (Loss)

The income (loss) of the golf shop is calculated by subtracting Total Departmental Expenses from Gross Profit on Golf Shop Revenue.

Country Club
Golf Course Maintenance—Schedule G

DEPARTMENTAL EXPENSES
    Payroll and related expenses $
        Salaries and wages
        Payroll taxes and employee benefits
        Employees' meals
            Total payroll and related expenses
    Other expenses
        Applicants
        Computer expense
        Dues and subscriptions
        Equipment rental
        Energy costs
        Fertilizer
        Gasoline and lubricants
        Laundry and linen
        Licenses and permits
        Operating supplies
        Printing and stationery
        Professional development
        Refuse removal
        Repairs and maintenance
            Course buildings
            Drainage systems
            Fences and bridges
            Irrigation systems
            Mowers, tractors and trucks
            Roads and paths
        Sand and top dressing
        Seeds, flowers and shrubs
        Small tools
        Telephone
        Topsoil
        Tree care
        Uniforms
        Vehicle expense
        Water
        Other operating expenses
            Total other expenses
TOTAL GOLF COURSE MAINTENANCE EXPENSES $

Note: This schedule is used for reporting the cost of maintaining the golf course. Grounds maintenance costs for other areas, other than racquet and aquatic sports, should be recorded in the facility maintenance department—see schedule R.

Golf Course Maintenance—Schedule G illustrates a format and identifies items that commonly appear on a supplementary schedule for the golf course maintenance department. This format and line items will vary according to the needs and requirements of individual clubs. Therefore, the line items listed on the schedule may not apply to golf course maintenance department of every club. Individual clubs should modify this schedule accordingly.

Departmental Expenses

Salaries and Wages

Salaries and Wages includes regular pay, overtime pay, vacation pay, sick pay, holiday pay, incentive pay, severance pay, and bonuses for employees of the golf course maintenance department. This line item should also include any expense associated with leased labor, but not contract labor, which should be charged to the relevant expense line item. If leased labor expense is significant, a separate line item called Leased Labor should be created and listed immediately after Salaries and Wages.

Payroll Taxes and Employee Benefits

Payroll Taxes and Employee Benefits includes payroll taxes, payroll-related insurance expense, retirement, and other payroll-related expenses applicable to the golf course maintenance department.

Employees' Meals

The cost of meals furnished to employees whose salaries and waged are charged to the golf course maintenance department is included in this expense item.

Total Payroll and Related Expenses

Total Payroll and Related Expenses is calculated by adding Salaries and Wages to Payroll Taxes and Employee Benefits and Employees' Meals.

Other Expenses

This expense grouping includes significant golf course maintenance department expenses. Items appearing under Other Expenses vary from club to club. Examples of items that commonly appear as Other Expenses follow:

Applicants. The cost of insecticides, pesticides, and similar chemicals used to maintain the golf course should be charged to this account.

Computer Expense. This item includes all expenses related to computer usage, including repairs and service contracts, supplies, and minor replacements. Major replacements should be capitalized and depreciated.

Dues and Subscriptions. This account should be charged with the cost of memberships, subscriptions to newspapers magazines, and books used by employees in golf course maintenance department.

Equipment Rental. The cost of equipment rented for use in the golf course maintenance department should be charged to this account.

Energy Costs. The cost of electricity and other energy used by the golf course maintenance department should be charged to this account.

Fertilizer. The cost of fertilizer should be charged to this account.

Gasoline and Lubricants. The cost of gasoline and lubricants for equipment used by the golf course maintenance department is charged to this account.

Laundry and Linen. This account should include the laundry costs assigned to this department.

Licenses and Permits. Licenses and Permits includes the cost of all licenses and permits required by the golf course maintenance department.

Operating Supplies. Operating Supplies includes the cost of cleaning supplies and similar operating expenses applicable to the golf course maintenance department. If the cost of any of these items is significant, items and amounts should be listed separately from Operating Supplies.

Printing and Stationery. This cost of printed forms, service manuals, stationery, and office supplies that are purchased from outside printers or produced internally should be charged to this account when they are used by employees of the golf course maintenance department.

Professional Development. Professional development includes costs other than time associated with training golf course maintenance employees. Examples include the costs of training materials, supplies, instructor fees, and outside seminars and conferences.

Refuse Removal. This account is used for recording the cost of waste removal.

Repairs and Maintenance. Several accounts will generally be used to record the repairs and maintenance of specific assets. The recommended accounts are course buildings; drainage systems; fences and bridges; irrigation systems; mowers, tractors and trucks; and roads and paths.

Sand and Top Dressing. The cost of sand and top dressing used on the golf course should be charged to this account.

Seeds, Flowers, and Shrubs. The cost of seeds, flowers, and shrubs used on the golf course should be charged to this account.

Small Tools. The cost of small tools such as rakes, shovels, etc. should be recorded in this account.

Telephone. Any telephone expenditures that can be directly related to the golf course maintenance department should be recorded in this account.

Topsoil. The cost of topsoil should be charged to this account.

Tree Care. The cost of maintaining trees on the golf course is recorded in this account. This also includes amounts paid to outsider contractors.

Uniforms. This item includes the cost or rental of uniforms for employees of the golf course maintenance department, as well as the cost of repairing uniforms of golf course maintenance department employees.

Vehicle Expense. The costs of operating and/or renting vehicles used by this department are recorded in this account.

Water. The cost of water purchased from outside sources for irrigating the golf course should be charged to this account.

Other Operating Expenses. This item includes costs of operating expenses applicable to the golf course maintenance department that do not apply to other line items discussed for this department.

Total Other Expenses

Total Other Expenses is calculated by adding all items listed under Other Expenses.

Total Golf Course Maintenance Department Expenses

Total Golf Course Maintenance Department Expenses is calculated by adding Total Payroll and Related Expenses to Total Other Expenses.

Country Club
Racquet Sports—Schedule H

REVENUE
    Court fees $
    Guest fees
    Rentals
    Tournament fees
    Other
        Total revenue   ———————

DEPARTMENTAL EXPENSES
    Payroll and related expenses
        Salaries and wages
        Payroll taxes and employee benefits
        Employees' meals   ———————
            Total payroll and related expenses   ———————
    Other expenses
        Computer expense
        Contract professionals
        Court maintenance
        Dues and subscriptions
        Energy costs
        Equipment rental
        Equipment repair and maintenance
        Gratis food
        Landscaping
        Laundry and linen
        Operating supplies
        Printing and stationery
        Prizes
        Professional development
        Telephone
        Tournament expenses
        Uniforms
        Vehicle expense
        Other operating expenses   ———————
            Total other expenses   ———————

TOTAL DEPARTMENTAL EXPENSES   ———————

DEPARTMENTAL INCOME (LOSS) $ ———————

Racquet Sports—Schedule H illustrates a format and identifies line items that commonly appear on a supplemental schedule for a club's racquet sports department. This format and the line items will vary according to the needs and requirements of individual clubs. Therefore, the line items listed on the schedule may not apply to racquet sports department of every club. Individual clubs should modify the schedule to meet their own needs and requirements. *Note:* When tournament activities are significant, a club may desire to show a separate schedule reflecting tournament revenues and expenses.

Revenue

Revenue includes court fees charged to members for the use of the courts, guest fees charged for the use of the courts by guests of members, revenue from the rental of tennis and other racquet equipment, fees charged for racquet tournaments, and any other revenues benefiting this department.

Departmental Expenses

Salaries and Wages

Salaries and Wages includes regular pay, overtime pay, vacation pay, sick pay, holiday pay, incentive pay, lessons and clinic pay, severance pay, and bonuses for employees of the racquet sports department. This line item should also include any expense associated with leased labor, but not contract labor, which should be charged to Contract Professionals or the relevant expense line item. If leased labor expense is significant, a separate line item called Leased Labor should be created and listed immediately after Salaries and Wages.

Payroll Taxes and Employee Benefits

Payroll Taxes and Employee Benefits includes payroll taxes, payroll-related insurance expense, retirement, and other payroll-related expenses applicable to the racquet sports department.

Employees' Meals

The cost of meals furnished to employees whose salaries and wages are charged to the racquet sports department is included in this expense item.

Total Payroll and Related Expenses

Total Payroll and Related Expenses is calculated by adding Salaries and Wages to Payroll Taxes and Employee Benefits and Employees' Meals.

Other Expenses

This expense grouping includes significant racquet sports expenses. Items appearing under Other Expenses vary from club to club. Examples of items that commonly appear as Other Expenses follow:

Computer Expense. This item includes all expenses related to computer usage, including repairs and service contracts, supplies, and minor replacements. Major replacements should be capitalized and depreciated.

Contract Professionals. Amounts paid to tennis and other racquet sports professionals under contract and not on the payroll should be charged to this account.

Court Maintenance. The expenses incurred to keep the courts in playable condition are charged to this account.

Dues and Subscriptions. This account should be charged with the cost of memberships, subscriptions to newspapers and magazines, and books used by racquet sports department employees.

Energy Expense. Electricity and other utilities, except water, used by the racquet sports department should be charged to this account.

Equipment Rental. The cost of equipment rented for use in the racquet sports department should be charged to this account.

Equipment Repair and Maintenance. This account is charged with the cost of materials used in maintaining and repairing equipment in the racquet sports department. The cost of work performed by outside contractors is also charged to this account.

Gratis Food. The cost of gratis food, including bottled water, provided to members and guests (not employees) interacting with the racquet sports department is charged to this account.

Landscaping. The cost of landscaping around the tennis courts should be charged to this account.

Laundry and Linen. This account should include the laundry costs assigned to this department.

Operating Supplies. Operating Supplies includes the cost of cleaning supplies, paper supplies (other than stationery), and similar operating expenses applicable to the racquet sports department. If the cost of any of these items is significant, items and amounts should be listed separately from Operating Supplies.

Printing and Stationery. This cost of printed forms, service manuals, stationery, and office supplies that are purchased from outside printers or produced internally should be charged to this account when they are used by employees of the racquet sports department.

Prizes. The cost of prizes awarded by the racquet sports department should be recorded in this account.

Professional Development. Professional development includes cost other than time associated with training racquet sports employees. Examples include the costs of training materials, supplies, instructor fees, and outside seminars and conferences.

Telephone. Any telephone expenditures that can be directly related to the racquet sports department should be charged to this account.

Tournament Expenses. All expenses incurred in administering tennis and other racquet sports tournaments should be charged to this account. *Note:* When tournament activities are significant, a club may desire to show a separate schedule reflecting tournament revenues and expenses.

Uniforms. This item includes the cost or rental of uniforms for employees of the racquet sports department, as well as the cost of repairing uniforms of racquet sports department employees.

Vehicle Expense. The costs of operating and/or renting vehicles used by this department are recorded in this account.

Other Operating Expenses. This item includes costs of operating expenses applicable to the racquet sports department that do not apply to other line items discussed for this department.

Total Other Expenses

Total Other Expenses is calculated by adding all items listed under Other Expenses.

Total Departmental Expenses

Total Departmental Expenses is calculated by adding Total Payroll and Related Expenses to Total Other Expenses.

Departmental Income (Loss)

The income (loss) of the racquet sports department is calculated by subtracting Total Departmental Expenses from Total Revenue.

Country Club
Racquet Shop—Schedule I

REVENUE $ _____

COST OF MERCHANDISE SOLD   _____
    Gross profit on racquet shop revenue   _____

DEPARTMENTAL EXPENSES
    Payroll and related expenses
        Salaries and wages
        Payroll taxes and employee benefits
        Employees' meals   _____
            Total payroll and related expenses   _____
    Other expenses
        Computer expense
        Contract services
        Dues and subscriptions
        Equipment rental
        Equipment repair and maintenance
        Gratis food
        Laundry and linen
        Operating supplies
        Printing and stationery
        Professional development
        Telephone
        Uniforms
        Other operating expenses   _____
            Total other expenses   _____

TOTAL DEPARTMENTAL EXPENSES   _____

DEPARTMENTAL INCOME (LOSS) $ _____

Racquet Shop—Schedule I illustrates a format and identifies line items that commonly appear on a supplemental schedule for a club's racquet shop when the club owns the shop. This format and the line items will vary according to the needs and requirements of individual clubs. Therefore, the line items listed on the schedule may not apply to racquet shop of every club. Individual clubs should modify the schedule to meet their own needs and requirements.

Revenue

Revenue is credited for sales of merchandise in the racquet shop. Allowances representing rebates and credits on racquet shop revenue should be charged directly against revenue.

Cost of Merchandise Sold

The Cost of Merchandise Sold represents the purchase price of merchandise sold in the racquet shop, less trade discounts (but not cash discounts), plus transportation, storage, and delivery charges. The amount may be derived by taking the value of inventory at the beginning of the period, adding total purchases, and subtracting ending inventory.

Gross Profit on Racquet Shop Revenue

This is determined by subtracting Cost of Merchandise Sold from Revenue.

Departmental Expenses

Salaries and Wages

Salaries and Wages includes regular pay, overtime pay, vacation pay, sick pay, holiday pay, incentive pay, severance pay, and bonuses for employees assigned to the racquet shop. This line item should also include any expense associated with leased labor, but not contract labor, which should be charged to Contract Services or the relevant expense line item. If leased labor expense is significant, a separate line item called Leased Labor should be created and listed immediately after Salaries and Wages.

Payroll Taxes and Employee Benefits

Payroll Taxes and Employee Benefits includes payroll taxes, payroll-related insurance expense, retirement, and other payroll-related expenses applicable to the racquet shop.

Employees' Meals

The cost of meals furnished to employees whose salaries and wages are charged to the racquet shop is included in this expense item.

Total Payroll and Related Expenses

Total Payroll and Related Expenses is calculated by adding Salaries and Wages to Payroll Taxes and Employee Benefits and Employees' Meals.

Other Expenses

This expense grouping includes significant racquet shop expenses. Items appearing under Other Expenses vary from club to club. Examples of items that commonly appear as Other Expenses follow:

Computer Expense. This item includes all expenses related to computer usage, including repairs and service contracts, supplies, and minor replacements. Major replacements should be capitalized and depreciated.

Contract Services. Contract Services includes any expenses associated with an activity that is normally charged to the department, but is now outsourced. Examples include the cost of contracting outside companies to wash windows and clean carpets and rugs in the racquet shop.

Dues and Subscriptions. This account should be charged with the cost of memberships, subscriptions to newspapers and magazines, and books used by employees in the racquet shop.

Equipment Rental. The cost of equipment rented for use in the racquet shop should be charged to this account.

Equipment Repair and Maintenance. This account is charged with the cost of materials used in maintaining and repairing equipment in the racquet shop. The cost of work performed by outside contractors is also charged to this account.

Gratis Food. The cost of gratis food, including bottled water, provided to members and guests (not employees) interacting with the racquet shop is charged to this account.

Laundry and Linen. This account should include the laundry costs assigned to this department.

Operating Supplies. Operating Supplies includes the cost of cleaning supplies, paper supplies (other than stationery), and similar operating expenses applicable to the racquet shop. If the cost of any of these items is significant, items and amounts should be listed separately from Operating Supplies.

Printing and Stationery. This cost of printed forms, service manuals, stationery, and office supplies that are purchased from outside printers or produced internally should be charged to this account when they are used by employees of the racquet shop.

Professional Development. Professional development includes cost other than time associated with training racquet shop employees. Examples include the costs of training materials, supplies, instructor fees, and outside seminars and conferences.

Telephone. Any telephone expenditures that can be directly related to the racquet shop should be charged to this account.

Uniforms. This item includes the cost or rental of uniforms for employees of the racquet shop, as well as the cost of repairing uniforms of racquet shop employees.

Other Operating Expenses. This item includes costs of operating expenses applicable to the racquet shop that do not apply to other line items discussed for this department.

Total Other Expenses

Total Other Expenses is calculated by adding all items listed under Other Expenses.

Total Departmental Expenses

Total Departmental Expenses is calculated by adding Total Payroll and Related Expenses to Total Other Expenses.

Departmental Income (Loss)

The income (loss) of the racquet shop is calculated by subtracting Total Departmental Expenses from Gross Profit on Racquet Shop Revenue.

Country Club
Aquatic Sports—Schedule J

REVENUE
Guest fees $
Rentals
Revenue from services
Other   _____
    Total revenue   _____

DEPARTMENTAL EXPENSES
Payroll and related expenses
    Salaries and wages
    Payroll taxes and employee benefits
    Employees' meals   _____
        Total payroll and related expenses   _____
Other expenses
    Chemicals
    Computer expense
    Contract professionals
    Dues and subscriptions
    Energy costs
    Equipment rental
    Equipment repairs and maintenance
    Gratis food
    Laundry and linen
    Licenses and permits
    Operating supplies
    Printing and stationery
    Prizes
    Professional development
    Telephone
    Uniforms
    Water
    Other operating expenses   _____
        Total other expenses   _____

TOTAL DEPARTMENTAL EXPENSES   _____

DEPARTMENTAL INCOME (LOSS) $ _____

Aquatic Sports—Schedule J illustrates a format and identifies line items that commonly appear on a supplemental schedule for the aquatic sports department. This format and the line items will vary according to the needs and requirements of individual clubs. Therefore, the line items listed on the schedule may not apply to aquatic sports departments of every club. Individual clubs should modify the schedule to meet their own needs and requirements.

Revenue

Revenue includes fees charged for use of aquatic facilities by guests of members; revenue derived from rental of lockers, mats, lounges, towels, etc.; fees charged for swimming instruction; and any other revenue of the aquatic sports department.

Departmental Expenses

Salaries and Wages

Salaries and Wages includes regular pay, overtime pay, vacation pay, sick pay, holiday pay, incentive pay, lessons and clinic fees, severance pay, and bonuses for employees of the aquatic sports department. This line item should also include any expense associated with leased labor, but not contract labor, which should be charged to Contract Professionals or the relevant expense line item. If leased labor expense is significant, a separate line item called Leased Labor should be created and listed immediately after Salaries and Wages.

Payroll Taxes and Employee Benefits

Payroll Taxes and Employee Benefits includes payroll taxes, payroll-related insurance expense, retirement, and other payroll-related expenses applicable to the aquatic sports department.

Employees' Meals

The cost of meals furnished to employees whose salaries and wages are charged to the aquatic sports department is included in this expense item.

Total Payroll and Related Expenses

Total Payroll and Related Expenses is calculated by adding Salaries and Wages to Payroll Taxes and Employee Benefits and Employees' Meals.

Other Expenses

This expense grouping includes significant aquatic sports department expenses. Items appearing under Other Expenses vary from club to club. Examples of items that commonly appear as Other Expenses follow:

Chemicals. The cost of chemicals used by the aquatic sports department should be recorded in this account.

Computer Expense. This item includes all expenses related to computer usage, including repairs and service contracts, supplies, and minor replacements. Major replacements should be capitalized and depreciated.

Contract Professionals. Amounts paid to swimming professionals under contract and not on the payroll of the club should be charged to this account.

Dues and Subscriptions. This account should be charged with the cost of memberships, subscriptions to newspapers and magazines, and books used by employees in the aquatic sports department.

Energy Costs. The cost of energy related to the aquatic sports department should be recorded in this account.

Equipment Rental. The cost of equipment rented for use in the aquatic sports department should be charged to this account.

Equipment Repair and Maintenance. This account is charged with the cost of materials used in maintaining and repairing the pool, pump equipment, and pipes. The cost of work performed by outside contractors is also charged to this account.

Gratis Food. The cost of gratis food, including bottled water, provided to members and guests (not employees) interacting with the aquatic sports department is charged to this account.

Laundry and Linen. This account should include both the laundry costs assigned to this department and the cost of towels and other linen purchased or rented for use by the aquatic sports department.

Licenses and Permits. Licenses and Permits includes the costs of all licenses and permits for the aquatic sports department.

Operating Supplies. Operating Supplies includes the cost of cleaning supplies, paper supplies (other than stationery), and similar operating expenses applicable to the aquatic sports department. If the cost of any of these items is significant, items and amounts should be listed separately from Operating Supplies.

Printing and Stationery. The cost of printed forms, service manuals, stationery, and office supplies that are purchased from outside printers or produced internally should be charged to this account when they are used by employees of the aquatic sports department.

Prizes. The cost of prizes awarded by the aquatic sports department should be recorded in this account.

Professional Development. Professional development includes costs other than time associated with training aquatic sports department employees. Examples include the costs of training materials, supplies, instructor fees, and outside seminars and conferences.

Telephone. Any telephone expenditures that can be directly related to the aquatic sports department should be charged to this account.

Uniforms. This item includes the cost or rental of uniforms for employees of the aquatic sports department, as well as the cost of repairing uniforms of aquatic sports department employees.

Water. The cost of water used in the swimming pool is charged to this account. An estimate of the cost should be made if there is not separate meter.

Other Operating Expenses. This item includes costs of operating expenses applicable to the aquatic sports department that do not apply to other line items discussed for this department.

Total Other Expenses

Total Other Expenses is calculated by adding all items listed under Other Expenses.

Total Departmental Expenses

Total Departmental Expenses is calculated by adding Total Payroll and Related Expenses to Total Other Expenses.

Departmental Income (Loss)

The income (loss) of the aquatic sports department is calculated by subtracting Total Departmental Expenses from Total Revenue.

City Club
Health and Fitness—Schedule K

REVENUE
    Activity fees $
    Guest fees
    Locker rentals
    Merchandise sales
    Other fees and services   _____
        Total revenue   _____

    Cost of merchandise sold   _____
        Gross profit on health and fitness revenue

DEPARTMENTAL EXPENSES
    Payroll and related expenses
        Salaries and wages
        Payroll taxes and employee benefits
        Employees' meals   _____
            Total payroll and related expenses   _____
    Other expenses
        Athletic supplies
        Computer expense
        Contract services
        Dues and subscriptions
        Equipment rental
        Equipment repairs and maintenance
        Gratis food
        Laundry and linen
        Operating supplies
        Printing and stationery
        Professional development
        Telephone
        Uniforms
        Other operating expenses   _____
            Total other expenses   _____

TOTAL DEPARTMENTAL EXPENSES   _____

DEPARTMENTAL INCOME (LOSS) $ _____

Health and Fitness—Schedule K illustrates a format and identifies line items that commonly appear on a supplemental schedule for a club's health and fitness department. This format and the line items will vary according to the needs and requirements of individual clubs. Therefore, the line items listed on the schedule may not apply to health and fitness department of every club. Individual clubs should modify the schedule to meet their own needs and requirements.

Revenue

Activity Fees

This account should be credited with fees received from members for use of the health and fitness facilities.

Guest Fees

Fees received for guests of members for the use of the health and fitness facilities should be credited to this account.

Locker Rentals

Locker rental fees earned in the health and fitness department should be credited to this account.

Merchandise Sales

Revenue is credited for sales merchandise in the health and fitness department. Allowances or returned merchandise should be directly charged against revenue.

Other Fees and Services

Other fees and services from the health and fitness department not recorded in other revenue accounts should be recorded in this account. An example would be fees for personal trainers.

Cost of Merchandise Sold

The Cost of Merchandise Sold represents the purchase price of merchandise sold in the health and fitness department, less trade discounts (but not cash discounts), plus transportation, storage, and delivery charges. The amount may be derived by taking the value of inventory at the beginning of the period, adding total purchase, and subtracting ending inventory.

Gross Profit on Health and Fitness Revenue

This is determined by subtracting Cost of Merchandise Sold from Total Revenue.

Departmental Expenses

Salaries and Wages

Salaries and Wages includes regular pay, overtime pay, vacation pay, sick pay, holiday pay, incentive pay, severance pay, and bonuses for employees of the health and fitness department. This line item should also include any expense associated with leased labor, but not contract labor, which should be charged to Contract Services or the relevant expense line item. If leased labor expense is significant, a separate line item called Leased Labor should be created and listed immediately after Salaries and Wages.

Payroll Taxes and Employee Benefits

Payroll Taxes and Employee Benefits includes payroll taxes, payroll-related insurance expense, retirement, and other payroll-related expenses applicable to the health and fitness department.

Employees' Meals

The cost of meals furnished to employees whose salaries and wages are charged to the health and fitness department is included in this expense item.

Total Payroll and Related Expenses

Total Payroll and Related Expenses is calculated by adding Salaries and Wages to Payroll Taxes and Employee Benefits and Employees' Meals.

Other Expenses

This expense grouping includes significant health and fitness department expenses. Items appearing under Other Expenses vary from club to club. Examples of items that commonly appear as Other Expenses follow:

Athletic Supplies. The cost of athletic supplies used in the health and fitness department should be recorded in this account.

Computer Expense. This item includes all expenses related to computer usage, including repairs and service contracts, supplies, and minor replacements. Major replacements should be capitalized and depreciated.

Contract Services. Contract Services includes any expenses associated with an activity that is normally charged to the department, but is now outsourced. Examples include the cost of contracting outside companies to wash windows and clean carpets and rugs in the health and fitness department.

Dues and Subscriptions. This account should be charged with the cost of memberships, subscriptions to newspapers and magazines, and books used by employees in the health and fitness department.

Equipment Rental. The cost of equipment rented for use in the health and fitness department should be charged to this account.

Equipment Repairs and Maintenance. This account is charged with the cost of materials used in maintaining and repairing equipment in the health and fitness department. The cost of work performed by outside contractors is also charged to this account.

Gratis Food. The cost of gratis food, including bottled water, provided to members and guests (not employees) interacting with the health and fitness department is charged to this account.

Laundry and Linen. This account should include both the laundry costs assigned to this department and the cost of towels and other linen purchased or rented for use by the health and fitness department.

Operating Supplies. Operating Supplies includes the cost of cleaning supplies, paper supplies (other than stationery), and similar operating expenses applicable to the health and fitness department. If the cost of any of these items is significant, items and amounts should be listed separately from Operating Supplies.

Printing and Stationery. This cost of printed forms, service manuals, stationery, and office supplies that are purchased from outside printers or produced internally should be charged to this account when they are used by employees of the health and fitness department.

Professional Development. Professional development includes costs other than time associated with training health and fitness employees. Examples include the costs of training materials, supplies, instructor fees, and outside seminars and conferences.

Telephone. Any telephone expenditures that can be directly related to the health and fitness department should be charged to this account.

Uniforms. This item includes the cost or rental of uniforms for employees of the health and fitness department, as well as the cost of repairing uniforms of health and fitness department employees.

Other Operating Expenses. This item includes costs of operating expenses applicable to the health and fitness department that do not apply to other line items discussed for this department.

Total Other Expenses

Total Other Expenses is calculated by adding all items listed under Other Expenses.

Total Departmental Expenses

Total Departmental Expenses is calculated by adding Total Payroll and Related Expenses to Total Other Expenses.

Departmental Income (Loss)

The income (loss) of the health and fitness department is calculated by subtracting Total Departmental Expenses from Gross Profit on Health and Fitness Revenue.

Country Club
Locker Rooms—Schedule L

REVENUE
    Locker rentals $
    Other   _____
        Total revenue   _____

DEPARTMENTAL EXPENSES
    Payroll and related expenses
        Salaries and wages
        Payroll taxes and employee benefits
        Employees' meals   _____
            Total payroll and related expenses   _____
    Other expenses
        Computer expenses
        Dues and subscriptions
        Equipment repairs and maintenance
        Gratis food
        Laundry and linen
        Member supplies
        Operating supplies
        Printing and stationery
        Professional development
        Telephone
        Uniforms
        Other operating expenses   _____
           Total other expenses   _____

TOTAL DEPARTMENTAL EXPENSES   _____

DEPARTMENTAL INCOME (LOSS) $ _____

Locker Rooms—Schedule L illustrates a format and identifies line items that commonly appear on a supplemental schedule for a club's locker rooms department. This format and the line items will vary according to the needs and requirements of individual clubs. Therefore, the line items listed on the schedule may not apply to locker rooms department of every club. Individual clubs should modify the schedule to meet their own needs and requirements.

Revenue

Revenue is credited for locker rentals and other. Other includes shoeshine fees and sale of spikes net of costs.

Departmental Expenses

Salaries and Wages

Salaries and Wages includes regular pay, overtime pay, vacation pay, sick pay, holiday pay, incentive pay, severance pay, and bonuses for employees of the locker rooms department. This line item should also include any expense associated with leased labor, but not contract labor, which should be charged to the relevant expense line item. If leased labor expense is significant, a separate line item called Leased Labor should be created and listed immediately after Salaries and Wages.

Payroll Taxes and Employee Benefits

Payroll Taxes and Employee Benefits includes payroll taxes, payroll-related insurance expense, retirement, and other payroll-related expenses applicable to the locker room department.

Employees' Meals

The cost of meals furnished to employees whose salaries and wages are charged to the locker rooms department is included in this expense item.

Total Payroll and Related Expenses

Total Payroll and Related Expenses is calculated by adding Salaries and Wages to Payroll Taxes and Employee Benefits and Employees' Meals.

Other Expenses

This expense grouping includes significant locker room expenses. Items appearing under Other Expenses vary from club to club. Examples of items that commonly appear as Other Expenses follow:

Computer Expense. This item includes all expenses related to computer usage, including repairs and service contracts, supplies, and minor replacements. Major replacements should be capitalized and depreciated.

Dues and Subscription. This account should be charged with the cost of memberships, subscriptions to newspapers and magazines, and books used by employees of the club's locker rooms.

Equipment Repair and Maintenance. This account is charged with the cost of materials used in maintaining and repairing equipment in the locker rooms. The cost of work performed by outside contractors is also charged to this account.

Gratis Food. The cost of gratis food, including bottled water, provided to members and guests (not employees) interacting with the locker rooms department is charged to this account.

Laundry and Linen. This account should include both the laundry costs assigned to this department and the cost of towels and other linen purchased or rented for use by the locker rooms department.

Member Supplies. The cost of member supplies should be charged to this account.

Operating Supplies. Operating Supplies includes the cost of cleaning supplies, paper supplies (other than stationery), and similar operating expenses applicable to the locker rooms. If the cost of any of these items is significant, items and amounts should be listed separately from Operating Supplies.

Printing and Stationery. This cost of printed forms, service manuals, stationery, and office supplies that are purchased from outside printers or produced internally should be charged to this account when they are used by employees of the locker rooms department.

Professional Development. Professional development includes cost other than time associated with training locker room employees. Examples include the costs of training materials, supplies, instructor fees, and outside seminars and conferences.

Telephone. Any telephone expenditures that can be directly related to the locker rooms should be charged to this account.

Uniforms. This item includes the cost or rental of uniforms for employees of the locker rooms department, as well as the cost of repairing uniforms of locker rooms department employees.

Other Operating Expenses. This item includes the cost of operating expenses applicable to locker rooms that do not apply to other line items discussed in this department.

Total Other Expenses

Total Other Expenses is calculated by adding all items listed under Other Expenses.

Total Departmental Expenses

Total Departmental Expenses is calculated by adding Total Payroll and Related Expenses to Total Other Expenses.

Departmental Income (Loss)

The income (loss) of the locker rooms department is calculated by subtracting Total Departmental Expenses from Total Revenue.

City or Country Club
Telecommunications—Schedule M

REVENUE	$ _____
COST OF CALLS	
Long-distance	
Local	
Rental of equipment	
Other	_____
Total cost of calls	_____
GROSS PROFIT ON TELECOMMUNICATIONS REVENUE	_____
DEPARTMENTAL EXPENSES	
Payroll and related expenses	
Salaries and wages	
Payroll taxes and employee benefits	
Employees' meals	_____
Total payroll and related expenses	_____
Other expenses	
Computer expense	
Dues and subscriptions	
Equipment rental	
Equipment repair and maintenance	
Operating supplies	
Printing and stationery	
Professional development	
Uniforms	
Other operating expenses	_____
Total other expenses	_____
TOTAL DEPARTMENTAL EXPENSES	_____
DEPARTMENTAL INCOME (LOSS)	$ _____

Telecommunications—Schedule M illustrates a format and identifies line items that commonly appear on a supplemental schedule for a telecommunications department. This format and the line items will vary according to the needs and requirements of individual clubs. Therefore, the line items listed on the schedule may not apply to telecommunications department of every club. Individual clubs should modify the schedule to meet their own needs and requirements.

Revenue

Revenue accounts should be credited with amounts charged to club members and their guests for using the club's telephones, Internet access, and related services. Further, commissions earned by the club should also be credited to revenue. A club may choose to report revenue in detail as follows: local calls, long distance calls, fax service, and commissions.

Cost of Calls

The Cost of Calls account should be charged with amounts telecommunications companies charge the club for telephone services. The club may choose to detail these charges to correspond to the detail shown for revenue.

Long-Distance/Local

The cost to the club of providing long-distance and local telecommunications services to members and guests should be charged to these accounts.

Rental of Equipment

The cost of renting telephone equipment is charged to this account.

Other

This item includes any cost of calls elements that do not apply to the above cost-of-call line items. An example would be utility taxes related to the revenue generated from resale of telecommunications services.

Gross Profit on Telecommunications Revenue

This is determined by subtracting Total Cost of Calls from Revenue.

Departmental Expenses

Salaries and Wages

Salaries and Wages includes regular pay, overtime pay, vacation pay, sick pay, holiday pay, incentive pay, severance pay, and bonuses for employees of the telecommunications department. This line item should also include any expense associated with leased labor, but not contract labor, which should be charged to the relevant expense line item. If leased labor expense is significant, a separate line item called Leased Labor should be created and listed immediately after Salaries and Wages.

Payroll Taxes and Employee Benefits

Payroll Taxes and Employee Benefits includes payroll taxes, payroll-related insurance expense, retirement, and other payroll-related expenses applicable to the telecommunications department.

Employees' Meals

The cost of meals furnished to employees whose salaries and wages are charged to the telecommunications department is included in this expense item.

Total Payroll and Related Expenses

Total Payroll and Related Expenses is calculated by adding Salaries and Wages to Payroll Taxes and Employee Benefits and Employees' Meals.

Other Expenses

This expense grouping includes significant telecommunications department expenses. Items appearing under Other Expenses vary from club to club. Examples of items that commonly appear as Other Expenses follow:

Computer Expense. This item includes all expenses related to computer usage, including repairs and service contracts, supplies, and minor replacements. Major replacements should be capitalized and depreciated.

Dues and Subscriptions. This account should be charged with the cost of memberships, subscriptions to newspapers and magazines, and books used by employees in the telecommunications department.

Equipment Rental. The cost of equipment rented for use by the telecommunications department (other than telephone equipment, which is addressed under Cost of Calls) should be charged to this account.

Equipment Repair and Maintenance. This account is charged with the cost of materials used in maintaining and repairing equipment in the telecommunication department. The cost of work performed by outside contractors is also charged to this account.

Operating Supplies. Operating Supplies includes the cost of cleaning supplies, paper supplies (other than stationery), and similar operating expenses applicable to the telecommunications department. If the cost of any of these items is significant, items and amounts should be listed separately from Operating Supplies.

Printing and Stationery. This cost of printed forms, service manuals, stationery, and office supplies that are purchased from outside printers or produced internally should be charged to this account when they are used by employees of the telecommunications department.

Professional Development. Professional development includes cost other than time associated with training telecommunications department employees. Examples include the costs of training materials, supplies, instructor fees, and outside seminars and conferences.

Uniforms. This item includes the cost or rental of uniforms for employees of the telecommunications department, as well as the cost of repairing uniforms of telecommunications department employees.

Other Operating Expenses. This item includes costs of operating expenses applicable to the telecommunications department that do not apply to line items discussed for this department.

Total Other Expenses

Total Other Expenses is calculated by adding all items listed under Other Expenses.

Total Departmental Expenses

Total Departmental Expenses is calculated by adding Total Payroll and Related Expenses to Total Other Expenses.

Departmental Income (Loss)

The income (loss) of the telecommunications department is calculated by subtracting Total Departmental Expenses from Gross Profit on Telecommunications Revenue.

City or Country Club
Other Operating Departments—Schedule N

REVENUE $ _____

COST OF MERCHANDISE SOLD _____
  Gross profit _____

DEPARTMENTAL EXPENSES
  Payroll and related expenses
    Salaries and wages
    Payroll taxes and employee benefits
    Employees' meals _____
      Total payroll and related expenses _____
  Other expenses
    Computer expense
    Contract services
    Dues and subscriptions
    Equipment rental
    Equipment repair and maintenance
    Gratis food
    Laundry and linen
    Operating supplies
    Printing and stationery
    Professional development
    Telephone
    Uniforms
    Other operating expenses _____
      Total other expenses _____

TOTAL DEPARTMENTAL EXPENSES _____

DEPARTMENTAL INCOME (LOSS) $ _____

Many clubs offer their services and/or merchandise to their members that are not provided by the operating departments discussed previously. In these cases, clubs must decide whether the sale of such services and/or merchandise will be done by operating departments within the facility or whether such operations will be contracted though rental or concession agreements. If a club decides to operate the sales of such services and/or merchandise, a separate schedule should be prepared for each of these areas of operations. Examples of other operating departments are as follows:

- Archery
- Badminton
- Bowling
- Children's Camp
- Croquet

- Curling

- Equestrian

- Gift/Apparel Shop

- Ice Skating

- Newsstand

- Skeet trapshooting

Other Operating Departments—Schedule N illustrates a format and identifies line items that commonly appear on a supplemental schedule for a club's other operating departments. This format and the line items will vary according to the needs and requirements of individual clubs. Therefore, the line items listed on the schedule may not apply to other operating departments of every club. Individual clubs should modify the schedule to meet their own needs and requirements.

Revenue

Revenue for any other operating department is derived from the sale of services and/or merchandise applicable to that department. Clubs may classify the items appearing under Revenue according to their individual needs and requirements. If, in relation to the total revenue generated by this department, a significant amount of revenue is generated by the sale of an item or by a group of similar items, the item or category should be listed separately under Revenue.

Cost of Merchandise Sold

The Cost of Merchandise Sold for other operating departments is calculated by adding the total purchases amount to the value of inventory at the beginning of the period and then subtracting the value of inventory at the end of the period. The total purchases amount is calculated by subtracting trade discounts (but not cash discounts) from the purchase price of merchandise and then adding transportation and delivery charges.

Gross Profit
This is determined by subtracting Cost of Merchandise Sold from Revenue.

Departmental Expenses

Salaries and Wages

Salaries and Wages includes regular pay, overtime pay, vacation pay, sick pay, holiday pay, incentive pay, severance pay, and bonuses for employees of other operating departments. This line item should also include any expense associated with leased labor, but not contract labor, which should be charged to Contract Services or the relevant expense line item. If leased labor expense is significant, a separate line item called Leased Labor should be created and listed immediately after Salaries and Wages.

Payroll Taxes and Employee Benefits

Payroll Taxes and Employee Benefits includes payroll taxes, payroll-related insurance expense, retirement, and other payroll-related expenses applicable to the other operating department.

Employees' Meals

The cost of meals furnished to employees whose salaries and wages are charged to the other operating department is included in this expense item.

Total Payroll and Related Expenses

Total Payroll and Related Expenses is calculated by adding Salaries and Wages to Payroll Taxes and Employee Benefits and Employees' Meals.

Other Expenses

This expense grouping includes significant other operating department expenses. Items appearing under Other Expenses vary from club to club. Examples of items that commonly appear as Other Expenses follow:

Computer Expense. This item includes all expenses related to computer usage, including repairs and service contracts, supplies, and minor replacements. Major replacements should be capitalized and depreciated.

Contract Services. Contract Services includes any expenses associated with an activity that is normally charged to the department, but is now outsourced. Examples include the cost of contracting outside companies to wash windows and clean carpets and rugs in the other operating department.

Dues and Subscriptions. This account should be charged with the cost of memberships, subscriptions to newspapers and magazines, and books used by employees in the other operating department.

Equipment Rental. The cost of equipment rented for use by the other operating department should be charged to this account.

Equipment Repair and Maintenance. This account is charged with the cost of materials used in maintaining and repairing equipment in the other operating department. The cost of work performed by outside contractors is also charged to this account.

Gratis Food. The cost of gratis food, including bottled water, provided to members and guests (not employees) interacting with the other operating department is charged to this account.

Laundry and Linen. This account should include both the laundry costs assigned to this department and the cost of towels and other linen purchased or rented for use by the other operating department.

Operating Supplies. Operating Supplies includes the cost of cleaning supplies, paper supplies (other than stationery), and similar operating expenses applicable to the other operating departments. If the cost of any of these items is significant, items and amounts should be listed separately from Operating Supplies.

Printing and Stationery. This cost of printed forms, service manuals, stationery, and office supplies that are purchased from outside printers or produced internally should be charged to this account when they are used by employees of other operating departments.

Professional Development. Professional development includes cost other than time associated with training other operating department employees. Examples include the costs of training materials, supplies, instructor fees, and outside seminars and conferences.

Telephone. Any telephone expenditures that can be directly related to the other operating department should be recorded in this account.

Uniforms. This item includes the cost or rental of uniforms for employees of other operating departments, as well as the cost of repairing uniforms of other operating department employees.

Other Operating Expenses. This item includes the cost of operating expenses applicable to the other operating departments that do not apply to line items discussed in other expense categories.

Total Other Expenses

Total Other Expenses is calculated by adding all items listed under Other Expenses.

Total Departmental Expenses

Total Departmental Expenses is calculated by adding Total Payroll and Related Expenses to Total Other Expenses.

Departmental Income (Loss)

The income (loss) of the other operating department is calculated by subtracting Total Departmental Expenses from Gross Profit.

City or Country Club
Rentals and Other Revenue—Schedule O

REVENUE
    Space rentals and concessions
    Commissions
    Cash discounts earned
    Interest income
    Other   _____
TOTAL RENTALS AND OTHER REVENUE $ _____

Rentals and Other Revenue—Schedule O illustrates a format and identifies line items that commonly appear on a supplemental schedule supporting rentals and other revenue of a club. This format and the line items will vary according to the needs and requirements of individual clubs. Therefore, the line items listed on the schedule may not apply to the rentals and other income operations of every club. Individual clubs should modify the schedule to meet their own needs and requirements.

Revenue

Space Rentals and Concessions

Many clubs offer services and/or merchandise to their members that are not provided by the operating departments previously discussed. In these cases, properties contract the operations of such activities through rental or concession agreements. Space Rentals and Concessions includes the revenue generated from the rental of space within the property. The space rented may house activities traditionally operated by a club itself as part of its usual member service offerings. Separate categories should be used to identify significant revenue items.

Commissions to renting agents should be amortized over the term of the leases and charged against the gross revenue from rentals. The schedule may include only the net rentals or, preferably, the gross rentals, commissions and expenses, and the resulting net rentals.

Commissions

This line item should be credited with commissions received from others for services, such as taxicab, garage and parking lot, and photography. Separate categories should be used to identify significant revenue items. Revenue from unowned games and vending machines would also be included here. So-called "commissions" from concessionaires should be included in the income from concessions.

Cash Discounts Earned

This account should be credited with the discount earned by the payment of creditors' accounts within the discount period, but should not be credited with trade discounts, which are more properly a deduction from cost of merchandise sold.

Interest Income

This account should be credited with interest earned on operating investments, bank deposits, notes receivable, accounts receivable, and from other sources. Any interest earned from non-operating investments should be shown separately under other activities on the Statement of Activities.

Other

This line item is used for revenue not shown on a separate line.

Total Rentals and Other Income

Total Rentals and Other Income is the sum of all items listed on this schedule.

City or Country Club
Administrative and General—Schedule P

DEPARTMENTAL EXPENSES
  Payroll and related expenses
    Salaries and wages $
    Payroll taxes and employee benefits
    Employees' meals   _____
      Total payroll and related expenses   _____
  Other expenses
    Bank charges
    Club publications
    Computer expense
    Credit and collection expenses
    Credit card fees
    Directors and committees
    Donations
    Dues and subscriptions
    Equipment rental
    Equipment repair and maintenance
    Licenses and permits
    Loss and damage
    Operating supplies and equipment
    Postage
    Printing and stationery
    Professional development
    Professional fees
    Provision for doubtful accounts
    Telephone
    Trade associations and conferences
    Uniforms
    Vehicle expense
    Website development and maintenance
    Other operating expenses   _____
      Total other expenses   _____
TOTAL ADMINISTRATIVE AND GENERAL EXPENSES $ _____

Administrative and General—Schedule P illustrates a format and identifies line items that commonly appear on the supplemental schedule for administrative and general expenses. These expenses are considered applicable to the entire club and are not easily allocated to operating departments. This format and the line items will vary according to the needs and requirements of individual clubs. Therefore, the line items listed on the schedule may not apply to the operations of every club. Individual clubs should modify the schedule to meet their own needs and requirements.

Departmental Expenses

Salaries and Wages

Salaries and Wages includes regular pay, overtime pay, vacation pay, sick pay, holiday pay, incentive pay, severance pay, and bonuses for employees of the administrative and general department. This line item should also include any expense associated with leased labor, but not the contract labor, which should be charged to the relevant expense line item. If leased labor expense is significant, a separate line item called Leased Labor should be created and listed immediately after Salaries and Wages.

Payroll Taxes and Employee Benefits

Payroll Taxes and Employee Benefits includes payroll taxes, payroll-related insurance expense, retirement, and other payroll-related expenses applicable to the administrative and general department.

Employees' Meals

The cost of meals furnished to employees whose salaries and wages are charged to the administrative and general department is included in this expense.

Total Payroll and Related Expenses

Total Payroll and Related Expenses is calculated by adding Salaries and Wages to Payroll Taxes and Employee Benefits and Employees' Meals.

Other Expenses

This expense grouping includes significant administrative and general department expenses. Items appearing under Other Expenses vary from club to club. Examples of items that commonly appear as Other Expenses follow:

Bank Charges. Bank charges assessed for miscellaneous banking services and transactions such as overdrafts, stop payments, check charges, and other related items should be charged to this account.

Club Publications. The cost of publishing club newsletters and similar publications should be charged to this account.

Computer Expense. The cost of management information systems services, supplies, and minor equipment should be charged to this account. In addition, this account includes the cost of software, peripheral equipment, and maintenance. To the extent practicable, these costs should be charged to user departments.

Credit Card Fees. This account is charged with the cost of credit card fees.

Credit and Collection of Expenses. This account is charged with the cost of collecting member accounts.

Directors and Committees. The costs associated with meetings of the club's directors and committees should be charged to this account.

Donations. Charitable contributions should be charged to this account.

Dues and Subscriptions. This account should be charged with the cost of memberships, subscriptions to newspapers and magazines, and books used by employees in the administrative and general department.

Equipment Rental. The cost of equipment rented for use by the administrative and general department should be charged to this account.

Equipment Repair and Maintenance. This account is charged with the cost of materials used in maintaining and repairing equipment in the administrative and general department. The cost of work performed by outside contractors is also charged to this account.

Licenses and Permits. The costs of licenses and permits of the club not charged to other departments of the club should be charged to this account.

Loss and Damage. Payments to members for property lost or damaged in excess of the amounts recovered from insurance companies are charged to this account. Also charged to this account are settlements of claims for damages.

Operating Supplies and Equipment. The cost of general office supplies such as adding machines, calculators, electric staplers, pencil sharpeners, and other similar equipment and related supplies, excluding equipment rental and capital items, should be charged to this account when used by, or purchased for, departments or employees whose salaries are charged to the administrative and general department.

Postage. This account is charged with the cost of postage attributable to the administrative and general department.

Printing and Stationery. The cost of printed forms and stationery supplies whether purchased from outside firms or produced internally should be charged to this account when used by the administrative and general department.

Professional Development. Professional development includes costs other than time associated with training administrative and general employees. Examples include the costs of training materials, supplies, instructor fees, and outside seminars and conferences.

Professional Fees. The cost of attorneys, public accountants, and professional consultants, including fees, travel, and other reimbursable expenses, should be charged to this account.

Provision for Doubtful Accounts. An amount sufficient to provide for the probable loss in collection of accounts receivable is charged to this account.

Telephone. Any telephone expenditures that can be directly related to the administrative and general department should be charged to this account.

Trade Associations and Conferences. Costs associated with club employees of the administrative and general department attending trade associations and conferences should be charged to this account. To the extent these conferences are for training, the costs should be charged to the professional development account.

Uniforms. This item includes the cost or rental of uniforms for employees of the administrative and general department, as well as the cost of repairing uniforms of administrative and general department employees.

Vehicle Expense. The costs of operating, maintaining, and renting vehicles used by the club's employees in the administrative and general department are charged to this account.

Website Development and Maintenance. The costs to develop and maintain the club's website should be charged to this account.

Other Operating Expenses. This item includes other costs applicable to the administrative and general department that do not apply to other line items discussed for this department.

Total Other Expenses

Total Other Expenses is calculated by adding all items listed under Other Expenses.

Total Administrative and General Expenses

Total Administrative and General Expenses is calculated by adding Total Payroll and Related Expenses to Total Other Expenses.

**City or Country Club
Clubhouse—Schedule Q**

DEPARTMENTAL EXPENSES
   Payroll and related expenses
      Salaries and wages $
      Payroll taxes and employee benefits
      Employees' meals
         Total payroll and related expenses   _____
   Other expenses
      Computer expense
      Contract services
      Dues and subscriptions
      Equipment rental
      Equipment repair and maintenance
      Gratis food
      Laundry and linen
      Library
      Member supplies
      Newspapers and periodicals
      Operating supplies
      Plants and decorations
      Printing and stationery
      Professional development
      Security
      Telephone
      Uniforms
      Vehicle expense
      Other operating expenses   _____
        Total other expenses   _____
TOTAL CLUBHOUSE EXPENSES $ _____

Clubhouse—Schedule Q illustrates a format and identifies line items that commonly appear on a supplemental schedule for a club's clubhouse. This schedule covers all the expenses for the main clubhouse in general and various other services to members that are not shown in any other department. This format and the line items will vary according to the needs and requirements of individual clubs. Therefore, the line items listed on this schedule may not apply to the clubhouse of every club. Individual clubs should modify this schedule to meet their own needs and requirements.

Departmental Expenses

Salaries and Wages

Salaries and Wages includes regular pay, overtime pay, vacation pay, sick pay, holiday pay, incentive pay, severance pay, and bonuses for employees assigned to the clubhouse. This line item should also include any expense associated with leased labor, but not the contract labor, which should be charged to the relevant expense line item. If leased labor expense is significant, a separate line item called Leased Labor should be created and listed immediately after Salaries and Wages.

Payroll Taxes and Employee Benefits

Payroll Taxes and Employee Benefits includes payroll taxes, payroll-related insurance expense, retirement, and other payroll-related expenses applicable to the clubhouse.

Employees' Meals

The cost of meals furnished to employees whose salaries and wages are charged to the clubhouse is included in this expense.

Total Payroll and Related Expenses

Total Payroll and Related Expenses is calculated by adding Salaries and Wages to Payroll Taxes and Employee Benefits and Employees' Meals.

Other Expenses

This expense grouping includes significant clubhouse expenses. Items appearing under Other Expenses vary from club to club. Examples of items that commonly appear as Other Expenses follow:

Computer Expense. This item includes all expenses related to computer usage, including repairs and service contracts, supplies, and minor replacements. Major replacements should be capitalized and depreciated.

Contract Services. Contract Services includes any expenses associated with an activity that is normally charged to the clubhouse, but is now outsourced. Examples include the cost of contracting outside companies to wash windows and clean carpets and rugs in the clubhouse.

Dues and Subscriptions. This account should be charged with the cost of memberships, subscriptions to newspapers and magazines, and books used by employees in the clubhouse.

Equipment Rental. The cost of equipment rented for use in the clubhouse should be charged to this account.

Equipment Repair and Maintenance. This account is charged with the cost of materials used in maintaining and repairing equipment in the clubhouse. The cost of work performed by outside contractors is also charged to this account.

Gratis Food. The cost of gratis food, including the cost of bottled water, provided to members and guests (not employees) interacting with the clubhouse is charged to this account.

Laundry and Linen. This account should include the laundry costs assigned to this department.

Library. The cost of reading material and other items in the club's library should be recorded in this account.

Member Supplies. The cost of supplies for the members' use in the clubhouse area of the club should be recorded in this account. Examples include matches and candy.

Newspapers and Periodicals. The cost of newspapers and periodicals provided for members' use should be recorded in this account.

Operating Supplies. Operating Supplies includes the cost of cleaning supplies, paper supplies (other than stationery), and similar operating expenses applicable to the clubhouse. If the cost of any of these items is significant, items and amounts should be listed separately from Operating Supplies.

Plants and Decorations. The cost of plants, fresh flowers, and other decorations for the clubhouse should be recorded in this account.

Printing and Stationery. This cost of printed forms, service manuals, stationery, and office supplies that are purchased from outside printers or produced internally should be charged to this account when they are used by employees of the clubhouse.

Professional Development. Professional development includes cost other than time associated with training clubhouse employees. Examples include the costs of training materials, supplies, instructor fees, and outside seminars and conferences.

Security. This account is used for recording the cost of security to the club. Examples would include security equipment, such as alarms and motion detectors, and contract security services including armored car services.

Telephone. Any telephone expenditures that can be directly related to the clubhouse should be charged to this account.

Uniforms. This item includes the cost or rental of uniforms for employees of the clubhouse, as well as the cost of repairing uniforms of clubhouse employees.

Vehicle Expense. The costs of operating, maintaining, and renting vehicles used by this department are recorded in this account.

Other Operating Expenses. This item includes costs of operating expenses applicable to the clubhouse that do not apply to other line items discussed for this department.

Total Other Expenses

Total Other Expenses is calculated by adding all items listed under Other Expenses.

Total Clubhouse Expenses

Total Clubhouse Expenses is calculated by adding Total Payroll and Related Expenses to Total Other Expenses.

City or Country Club
Facility Maintenance and Energy—Schedule R

DEPARTMENTAL EXPENSES
    Payroll and related expenses
        Salaries and wages $
        Payroll taxes and employee benefits
        Employees' meals   _____
            Total payroll and related expenses   _____
    Other expenses
        Building
        Computer expense
        Curtains and draperies
        Dues and subscriptions
        Electrical and mechanical equipment
        Elevators
        Equipment rental
        Floor coverings
        Furniture
        Grounds and landscaping
        HVAC
        Laundry and linen
        Operating supplies
        Painting and decorating
        Pest control
        Plumbing
        Printing and stationery
        Professional development
        Refuse removal
        Telephone
        Uniforms
        Vehicle expense
        Other operating expenses   _____
            Total other expenses   _____
TOTAL FACILITY MAINTENANCE EXPENSES $ _____

ENERGY COSTS
    Electricity $
    Fuel
    Other
    Steam
    Water   _____
TOTAL ENERGY COSTS $ _____

Facility Maintenance and Energy—Schedule R illustrates a format and identifies line items that commonly appear on the supplemental schedule for a club's facility maintenance department and energy. This format and the line items will vary according to the needs and requirements of individual clubs. Therefore, the line items listed on this schedule may not apply to the facility maintenance department and energy of every club. Individual clubs should modify this schedule to meet their own needs and requirements.

Departmental Expenses

Salaries and Wages

Salaries and Wages includes regular pay, overtime pay, vacation pay, sick pay, holiday pay, incentive pay, severance pay, and bonuses for employees of the facility maintenance department. This line item should also include any expense associated with leased labor, but not the contract labor, which should be charged to the relevant expense line item. If leased labor expense is significant, a separate line item called Leased Labor should be created and listed immediately after Salaries and Wages.

Payroll Taxes and Employee Benefits

Payroll Taxes and Employee Benefits includes payroll taxes, payroll-related insurance expense, retirement, and other payroll-related expenses applicable to the facility maintenance department.

Employees' Meals

The cost of meals furnished to employees whose salaries and wages are charged to the facility maintenance department is included in this expense.

Total Payroll and Related Expenses

Total Payroll and Related Expenses is calculated by adding Salaries and Wages to Payroll Taxes and Employee Benefits and Employees' Meals.

Other Expenses

This expense grouping includes significant facility maintenance department expenses. Items appearing under Other Expenses vary from club to club. Examples of items that commonly appear as Other Expenses follow:

Building. This account is charged with cost of material used and contracts related to repairing the building, both interior and exterior.

Computer Expense. This item includes all expenses related to computer usage, including repairs and service contracts, supplies, and minor replacements. Major replacements should be capitalized and depreciated.

Curtains and Draperies. This account is charged with the cost of materials used in repairing hangings and covers and the cost of work performed by outside firms.

Dues and Subscriptions. This account should be charged with the cost of memberships, subscriptions to newspapers and magazines, and books used by employees of the facility maintenance department.

Electrical and Mechanical Equipment. This account is charged with the cost of materials and contracts related to repairing and maintaining equipment not specifically identified elsewhere.

Elevators. This account is charged with the cost of repairing elevators and would include inspection service.

Floor Coverings. The cost of floor coverings should be charged to this account.

Furniture. This account is charged with the cost of materials (e.g., textiles, fibers, lumber, hardware, glass) used in repairing furniture and the cost of work performed by outside firms.

Grounds and Landscaping. The cost of supplies and contracts related to the maintenance of grounds not related to a specific operating department should be charged to this account.

HVAC. This line item should be charged with the cost of materials and contracts related to repairing and maintaining heating, ventilating, and air conditioning equipment.

Laundry and Linen. This account should include the laundry costs assigned to this department.

Operating Supplies. Operating Supplies includes the cost of cleaning supplies, paper supplies (other than stationery), and similar operating expenses applicable to the facility maintenance department. If the cost of any of these items is significant, items and amounts should be listed separately from Operating Supplies.

Painting and Decorating. This line item should be charged with the cost of materials, supplies, and related contracts for painting and decorating the clubhouse.

Pest Control. The cost of materials, supplies, and contract services used to control pests in the clubhouse and surrounding areas. Examples include rodent bait and traps. Contract services for specific departments should be assigned to those departments.

Plumbing. This account includes the cost of plumbing supplies used by the club.

Printing and Stationery. This cost of printed forms, service manuals, stationery, and office supplies that are purchased from outside printers or produced internally should be charged to this account when they are used by employees of the facility maintenance department.

Professional Development. This account includes cost of professional development other than time associated with training facility maintenance department employees. Examples include the costs of training materials, supplies, instructor fees, and outside seminars and conferences.

Refuse Removal. The cost of waste removal and incinerator operations is charged to this account.

Telephone. Any telephone expenditures that can be directly related to the facility maintenance department should be charged to this account.

Uniforms. This item includes the cost or rental of uniforms for employees of the facility maintenance department, as well as the cost of repairing uniforms of facility maintenance department employees.

Vehicle Expense. The cost to operate, maintain, and rent vehicles used by employees of the facility maintenance department should be charged to this account.

Other Operating Expenses. This item includes costs of operating expenses applicable to the facility maintenance department not falling under any other expense captions.

Total Other Expenses

Total Other Expenses is calculated by adding all items listed under Other Expenses.

Total Facility Maintenance Expenses

Total Facility Maintenance Expenses is calculated by adding Total Payroll and Related Expenses to Total Other Expenses.

Energy Costs

Electricity

The cost of light and power purchased from outside producers is charged to this account.

Fuel

This account includes the cost of fuel consumed, excluding kitchen fuel, which is charged to the food department. Fuel includes heating fuel, natural gas, and propane gas.

Steam

The cost of steam purchased from outside producers is charged to this account.

Water

This account is charged with the cost of water consumed and includes the cost of water specifically treated and water purchased for drinking purposes. The cost of water used on the golf course and swimming pool should be charged to Schedules G and J, respectively.

Other

This account is for expenses not falling under any of the designated categories.

Total Energy Costs

Total Energy Costs is calculated by adding all items listed under Energy Costs.

City or Country Club
Fixed Charges and Income Taxes—Schedule S

RENT, PROPERTY TAXES AND OTHER MUNICIPAL CHARGES, AND INSURANCE
Rent
    Real estate rental (land and buildings) $ _____
    Other rentals
      Total   _____
Property taxes and other municipal charges
    Real estate taxes
    Personal property taxes
    Business taxes
    Other   _____
      Total   _____
Insurance   _____
TOTAL RENT, PROPERTY TAXES AND OTHER MUNICIPAL CHARGES, AND INSURANCE   _____

INTEREST EXPENSE
Mortgage payable
Notes payable
Obligations under capital leases
Other long-term debt
Other interest   _____
TOTAL INTEREST EXPENSE   _____

DEPRECIATION AND AMORTIZATION
Golf course improvements
Leaseholds and leasehold improvements
Building and improvements
Furnishings, fixtures and equipment
Other   _____
TOTAL DEPRECIATION AND AMORTIZATION   _____

FEDERAL AND STATE INCOME TAXES
Federal
    Current
    Deferred   _____
      Total federal income taxes   _____
State
    Current
    Deferred   _____
      Total state income taxes   _____
TOTAL FEDERAL AND STATE INCOME TAXES $ _____

Fixed Charges and Income Taxes—Schedule T details the expenses incurred by a club for rent, property taxes, insurance, depreciation and amortization, and income taxes.

Rent, Property Taxes and Other Municipal Charges, and Insurance

Rent

Real Estate Rental (Land and Buildings). If club property is leased, this account is charged with the amount of the rental.

Other Rentals. This includes the rental cost of major items other than land and buildings which, if not rented, would be purchased and capitalized as fixed assets (excluding telephone equipment). Rental of miscellaneous equipment (e.g., copiers, projectors, sound equipment) for a specific function, such as a banquet, are to be charged to the appropriate department and not charged to this account.

Property Taxes and Other Municipal Charges

Real Estate Taxes. This account is charged with all taxes assessed against the real property of the club by a state or political subdivision of a state. Assessments for public improvements are not to be included in this account, but should be capitalized as fixed assets.

Personal Property Taxes. If material, personal property taxes should be shown separately.

Business Taxes. Business taxes (such as gross receipts taxes on sales of rooms, food and beverage) that cannot be passed on to members are charged to this account.

Other. This account refers to all other taxes, excluding income taxes and payroll taxes. If material, the taxes should be separately identified.

Insurance

This account should be used to record the cost of insuring the club building and contents against damage or destruction by fire, weather, sprinkler leakage, boiler explosion, plate glass breakage, etc. In addition, general insurance costs, including premiums related to directors' and officers' liability, fidelity bonds, and theft coverage should be charged to this account. Payroll-related insurance costs such as workers' compensation and social insurance are included in Payroll Taxes and Employee Benefits in the appropriate department schedule to which the associated payroll is charged.

Total Rent, Property Taxes and Other Municipal Charges, and Insurance. This total is calculated by summing the total rent, total property taxes and municipal charges and insurance costs.

Interest Expense

This account is charged with interest expense on obligations such as: mortgage payable, notes payable, obligations under capital leases, other long-term debt, and other indebtedness on which interest is charged. Interest charges should be grouped into categories which indicate the source of the indebtedness to which they relate.

Depreciation and Amortization

Golf Course Improvements

Depreciation of these items is charged to this account over the estimated lives of the assets.

Leaseholds and Leasehold Improvements

Amortization of the costs of acquiring a leasehold is charged to this account over the life of the related lease. Amortization of the costs of acquiring leasehold improvements is charged to this account over either the life of the lease or the life of the improvement, whichever is less.

Buildings and Improvements

Depreciation on the club building(s) and improvements are charged to this account over the estimated lives of these assets.

Furniture, Fixtures, and Equipment

Depreciation of these items is charged to this account over the estimated lives of the assets. The account should not include, however, depreciation of items (e.g., china, glassware, silver, linen, uniforms) accounted by the inventory method and charged to a particular department.

Other

The amortization of intangibles and other depreciation and amortization of other long-term assets that are not included in the above categories should be charged to this line item.

Federal and State Income Taxes

Taxes assessed on the basis of nonmember related or passive income earned by the club are charged to this account. When differences exist between income reported for financial statement purposes and for income tax purposes, the amount of tax currently payable and the deferred amount should be shown separately.

City or Country Club
House Laundry—Schedule T

DEPARTMENTAL EXPENSES
    Payroll and related expenses
        Salaries and wages $
        Payroll taxes and employee benefits
        Employees' meals   _____
            Total payroll and related expenses   _____
    Other expenses
        Computer expense
        Dues and subscriptions
        Equipment rental
        Equipment repair and maintenance
        Laundry supplies
        Operating supplies
        Printing and stationery
        Professional development
        Uniforms
        Other operating expenses   _____
            Total other expenses   _____

TOTAL DEPARTMENTAL EXPENSES   _____
    Credits
        Member and guest laundry
        Concessionaire laundry   _____
            Total credits   _____

COST OF HOUSE LAUNDRY $ _____

CHARGED TO OTHER DEPARTMENTS
    Food
    Beverage
    Entertainment
    Overnight rooms
    Golf operations
    Golf shop
    Golf course maintenance
    Racquet sports
    Racquet shop
    Aquatic sports
    Health and fitness
    Locker rooms
    Other operating departments
    Clubhouse
    Facility maintenance and energy   _____
        Total charged to other departments $ _____

House Laundry—Schedule T illustrates a format and identifies line items that commonly appear on a supplemental schedule for a club's house laundry. This format and the line items will vary according to the needs and requirements of individual cubs. Therefore, the line items listed on this schedule may not apply to house laundry of every club. Individual clubs should modify the schedule to meet their own needs and requirements.

Departmental Expenses

Salaries and Wages

Salaries and Wages includes regular pay, overtime pay, vacation pay, sick pay, holiday pay, incentive pay, severance pay, and bonuses for employees of the house laundry. This line item should also include any expense associated with leased labor, but not contract labor, which should be charged to the relevant expense line item. If leased labor expense is significant, a separate line item called Leased Labor should be created and listed immediately after Salaries and Wages.

Payroll Taxes and Employee Benefits

Payroll Taxes and Employee Benefits includes payroll taxes, payroll-related insurance expense, retirement, and other payroll-related expenses applicable to the house laundry.

Employees' Meals

The cost of meals furnished to employees whose salaries and wages are charged to the house laundry is included in this expense item.

Total Payroll and Related Expenses

Total Payroll and Related Expenses is calculated by adding Salaries and Wages to Payroll Taxes and Employee Benefits and Employees' Meals.

Other Expenses

This expense grouping includes significant house laundry expenses. Items appearing under Other Expenses vary from club to club. Examples of items that commonly appear as Other Expenses follow:

Computer Expense. This item includes all expenses related to computer usage, including repairs and service contracts, supplies, and minor replacements. Major replacements should be capitalized and depreciated.

Dues and Subscriptions. This account should be charged with the cost of memberships, subscriptions to newspapers and magazines, and books used by employees in the house laundry.

Equipment Rental. The cost of equipment rented for use in the house laundry should be charged to this account.

Equipment Repair and Maintenance. This account is charged with the cost of materials used in maintaining and repairing items in the house laundry. The cost of work performed by outside contractors is also charged to this account.

Laundry Supplies. Examples of items to be included in this group would be any items used for laundering purposes and items used for wrapping, etc., if appropriate.

Operating Supplies. Operating Supplies includes the cost of cleaning supplies, paper supplies (other than stationery), and similar operating expenses applicable to the house laundry. If the cost of any of these items is significant, items and amounts should be listed separately from Operating Supplies.

Printing and Stationery. This cost of printed forms, service manuals, stationery, laundry lists, and office supplies that are purchased from outside printers or produced internally should be charged to this account when they are used by employees of the house laundry.

Professional Development. Professional development includes costs other than time associated with training house laundry employees. Examples include the costs of training materials, supplies, instructor fees, and outside seminars and conferences.

Uniforms. This item includes the cost or rental of uniforms for employees of house laundry, as well as the cost of repairing uniforms of house laundry employees.

Other Operating Expenses. This item includes costs of other expenses applicable to the house laundry that do not apply to any other line items for this department.

Total Other Expenses

Total Other Expenses is calculated by adding all items listed under Other Expenses.

Total Departmental Expenses

Total Departmental Expenses is calculated by adding the Total Payroll and Related Expenses to Total Other Expenses.

Credits

Member and Guest Laundry

This account is credited with amounts charged to members and guests receiving laundry services.

Concessionaire Laundry

Where laundering is done for concessionaires such as barber/beauty shops, the revenue received is generally deducted from the total expenses of this department.

Cost of House Laundry

Cost of House Laundry is calculated by subtracting Total Credits from Total Departmental Expenses.

Charged to Other Departments

The Cost of House Laundry is distributed to all the club's departments using laundry services. This cost appears on the appropriate schedules under Laundry and Linen.

```
┌─────────────────────────────────────────────────────────────────────────┐
│                          City or Country Club                             │
│              Payroll Taxes and Employee Benefits—Schedule U               │
│                                                                           │
│  PAYROLL TAXES                                                            │
│     Federal retirement (FICA)                              $              │
│     Federal unemployment (FUTA)                                           │
│     Medicare (FICA)                                                       │
│     State disability                                                      │
│     State unemployment (SUTA)                          _____      │
│        Total payroll taxes                             _____      │
│                                                                           │
│  EMPLOYEE BENEFITS                                                        │
│     Auto allowance                                                        │
│     Child care                                                            │
│     Dental insurance                                                      │
│     Disability insurance                                                  │
│     Group life insurance                                                  │
│     Health insurance                                                      │
│     Meals                                                                 │
│     Nonunion insurance                                                    │
│     Nonunion retirement                                                   │
│     Retirement plan                                                       │
│     Union insurance                                                       │
│     Union retirement                                                      │
│     Workers' compensation insurance                                       │
│     Other                                              _____      │
│        Total employee benefits                         _____      │
│  TOTAL PAYROLL TAXES AND EMPLOYEE BENEFITS             $ _____      │
└─────────────────────────────────────────────────────────────────────────┘
```

Payroll Taxes and Employee Benefits—Schedule U illustrates one format and identifies line items that commonly appear on a supplemental schedule supporting the payroll taxes and employee benefits. An alternative format for this schedule is presented in Appendix E. The line items on either format will vary according to the needs and requirements of individual clubs. Therefore, the line items listed may not apply to the operations of every club. Individual clubs should modify the chosen schedule to meet their own needs and requirements.

Payroll Taxes

Federal (FICA)

This account is to be charged with taxes imposed on clubs by Subchapter B, Chapter 21, of the Internal Revenue Code.

Federal Unemployment (FUTA)

This account is to be charged with contributions by clubs by Subchapter D, Chapter 21, of the Internal Revenue Code.

Medicare (FICA)

This account is to be charged with taxes imposed by Chapter 25 of the Internal Revenue Code.

State Disability

This account is to be charged with contributions by clubs to state agencies for disabilities purposes.

State Unemployment (SUTA)

This account is to be charged with contributions by employers to unemployment funds required by state unemployment compensation laws.

Employee Benefits

Auto Allowance

This account is charged with the cost of providing payment to employees for allowances for use of their autos.

Child Care

This account is charged with the cost of providing contracted care or in-house facilities for employees' children.

Dental Insurance

This account is charged with the employer costs of dental insurance for employees less amounts reimbursed. This should be shown net of the employee contribution.

Disability Insurance

This account is charged with the cost of providing disability insurance for employees.

Group Life Insurance

This account is charged with the cost of group life insurance on employees.

Health Insurance

This account is charged with the club cost of health insurance for employees. This should be shown net of the employee contribution.

Meals

This account is charged with the club cost of providing meals to employees.

Nonunion Insurance

This account is charged with the cost of life, health, accident, hospitalization, and other insurance for employees not participating in a union fund.

Nonunion Retirement

This account is charged with the costs associated with nonunion retirement plans.

Retirement Plan

This account is charged with the cost of a club's portion of programs with matching amounts and administrative costs.

Union Insurance

This account is charged with the costs associated with union employees' benefit funds for insurance on life, health, accident, hospitalization, and other purposes.

Union Retirement

This account is charged with the costs associated with union employees' retirement benefit funds.

Workers' Compensation Insurance

This account is charged with the cost of insurance for employee state compensation plans.

Other

This account is charged with the cost of providing employees with other benefits not included under other captions (e.g., daytimers, name tags, organization dues, employee award and incentive parties, etc.).

Appendix A
Financial Statement Formats

The latest accounting and spreadsheet programs have greatly facilitated the generation of more complex financial statement formats. Most accounting programs have multiple report formats that allow the user to create a myriad of reports showing comparisons by dollar and percentage. Users should modify their reports to meet the needs and requirements of their clubs. Relevance is greatly enhanced by adding columns to provide:

- A comparative analysis of the current period results with the amounts budgeted for the period.

- A comparative analysis of the current period results with those of the same period for the preceding year.

- Cumulative year-to-date information.

- Percentage relationships between revenue and expenses.

Comparisons may be made horizontally or vertically. Horizontal analysis compares the dollar (absolute) and percentage (relative) differences between two amounts of the same line items—for example, laundry as a dollar and percentage this year compared with laundry as a dollar and percentage last year or with budget. Vertical analysis expresses revenue and expenses as percentages of net revenue by using net revenue as the common denominator. Vertical analysis is very common in food and beverage areas. Identifying labor and cost of sales as a percentage of revenues is a benchmark monitored closely by most managers.

Many formats are possible. Two examples are presented on the following page.

Alternative Format A includes columns for both current period and year-to-date information for actual and comparative figures. The comparative figures may be budget or the results of the same period for the preceding year. A comparison with budget or forecast is preferred since this enables management to concentrate on the underlying business reasons that actual results exceeded or fell short of planned results. Comparisons with previous periods are useful for indicating the relative performance of current operations.

Alternative Format B is for those clubs desiring a presentation that includes actual, budgeted, and prior-year information for both the current period and the year to date. In addition, columns have been provided to show the dollar variance between actual results and the budget. Significant variances warrant an explanation by notes accompanying the financial statements or comments inserted into the documents.

Alternative Format A

Description	Current Month					Year-To-Date				
	Actual		Comparative			Actual		Comparative		
	Dollars	Percent	Dollars	Percent		Dollars	Percent	Dollars	Percent	

Alternative Format B

Description	Current Month							Year-To-Date						
	Actual		Budget			Prior Year		Actual		Budget			Prior Year	
	Dollars	Percent	Dollars	Percent	Variance	Dollars	Percent	Dollars	Percent	Dollars	Percent	Variance	Dollars	Percent

Appendix B
Ratio Analysis and Statistics

The use of ratios and statistics as a basis of comparison, measurement, and communication is prevalent within the club industry. The usefulness of these tools is predicated on a commonality of definition and understanding. The various ratios and statistics that can be developed and be useful are numerous. The intent of this appendix is to provide a consistent, uniform definition of basic club industry ratios and statistics. This section includes only a few ratios and statistics that are in widespread general use within the industry. It is not intended to be a complete listing and definition of all possible relevant ratios and statistics.

Ratio Analysis

Financial statements issued by club properties contain a considerable amount of information. A thorough analysis of this information requires more than simply reading the reported figures and facts. Users of financial statements need to be able to interpret the figures and facts, and make them yield information that reveals aspects of the club's financial situation or operation that could otherwise go unnoticed. This is accomplished through ratio analysis, which compares related facts reported on financial statements. A ratio gives mathematical expression to a relationship between two figures, and is calculated by dividing one figure by the other.

Although ratios are critical to any financial analysis, they are only indicators and, as indicators, they are meaningful only when compared with useful criteria. Useful criteria with which to compare the results of ratio analysis include:

- The corresponding ratio calculated for a prior period
- Other clubs and industry averages
- Planned ratio goals

Users of ratio analysis must be careful when comparing two different clubs, because the accounting procedures used by the clubs may differ and their ratios may not be comparable. Ratio analysis can be extremely useful to board members, committee chairs, creditors, and managers in evaluating the financial condition and operation of a club. However, ratios do not resolve problems or actually reveal what the problems may be. At best, when ratios vary significantly from past periods, budgeted standards, or industry averages, they indicate that problems may exist. When problems appear to exist, considerably more analysis and investigation are necessary to determine the appropriate corrective actions.

Liquidity Ratios

Liquidity ratios measure a club's ability to meet its current, short-term obligations. Creditors normally prefer relatively high liquidity ratios because this gives them assurance that the club will be able to meet its short-term obligations. Management desires to maintain adequate working capital and sufficient liquidity to ensure the smooth operations of the club, but realizes longer term investments produce higher financial returns.

Current Ratio

The most common liquidity ratio is the current ratio, which is the ratio of total current assets to total current liabilities. The current ratio can be calculated as follows:

$$\text{Current Ratio} = \frac{\text{Current Assets}}{\text{Current Liabilities}}$$

This ratio reveals the amount of current assets for every dollar of current liabilities.

Acid-Test Ratio

The acid-test ratio measures a club's liquidity by considering only "quick assets"—current assets minus inventories, prepaid expenses, and other current assets. This is often a more stringent measure of a club's liquidity because it may take a few months for many clubs to convert their inventories to cash. The acid-test ratio can be calculated as follows:

$$\text{Acid-Test Ratio} = \frac{\text{Quick Assets}}{\text{Current Liabilities}}$$

Accounts Receivable Turnover

Accounts receivable is often the largest current asset of a club because credit is extended to members. Therefore, any examination of a club's liquidity must consider how quickly accounts receivable are converted to cash. This is determined by the accounts receivable turnover ratio, which divides total revenue by the average accounts receivable.

To calculate the accounts receivable turnover, it is first necessary to determine the average accounts receivable. This is accomplished by adding accounts receivable at the beginning and end of the period and then dividing that figure by two. The average accounts receivable figure is then divided into the total revenue for the period. The accounts receivable turnover can be calculated as follows:

$$\text{Accounts Receivable Turnover} = \frac{\text{Total Revenue}}{\text{Average Accounts Receivable}}$$

Average Collection Period

This ratio reveals the number of days required to collect the average accounts receivable. The average collection period is calculated by dividing the number of days in the year by the accounts receivable turnover. The average collection period for the year can be calculated as follows:

$$\text{Average Collection Period} \quad = \quad \frac{\text{Days in Year}}{\text{Accounts Receivable Turnover}}$$

Solvency Ratios

Solvency ratios measure the degree of financing used. These ratios reflect the ability of the club to meet its long-term obligations. Owners (members) of many clubs prefer their club to use debt to finance expansion and replacements. Creditors prefer relatively high solvency ratios because they reveal an equity cushion available to absorb any operating losses. Management in some clubs is caught in the middle, trying to satisfy members by financing assets so as to minimize investments of members and trying to satisfy creditors by not unduly jeopardizing the club's ability to meet its long-term obligations.

Solvency Ratio

A club is solvent when its assets are greater than its liabilities. The solvency ratio compares total assets to total liabilities. The solvency ratio can be calculated as follows:

$$\text{Solvency Ratio} \quad = \quad \frac{\text{Total Assets}}{\text{Total Liabilities}}$$

This ratio reveals the amount of assets for every dollar of liabilities.

Debt-Equity Ratio

One of the most common solvency ratios is the debt-equity ratio, which compares the total debt of the club to the total investment in the operation by the members.

$$\text{Debt-Equity Ratio} = \frac{\text{Total Liabilities}}{\text{Total Members' Equity}}$$

This ratio reveals the amount owed to creditors for every dollar of net assets.

Number of Times Interest Earned

This ratio expresses the number of times interest expense can be covered. The greater the number of times interest is earned, the greater the safety afforded creditors. The number of times interest earned ratio can be calculated as follows:

$$\begin{array}{c}\text{Number of Times} \\ \text{Interest Earned Ratio}\end{array} \quad = \quad \frac{\begin{array}{c}\text{Income Before Income Taxes} \\ \text{+ Interest Expense}\end{array}}{\text{Interest Expense}}$$

Clubs that obtain the use of property and equipment through leases may find the fixed charge coverage ratio to be more useful than the number of times interest earned ratio.

Fixed Charge Coverage Ratio

This ratio is a variation of the number of times interest earned ratio and is useful for those clubs that have long-term operating leases that require periodic payments similar to interest expense. Lease expense is added to both the numerator and denominator of the number of times interest earned ratio. The fixed charge coverage ratio can be calculated as follows:

$$\text{Fixed Charge Coverage Ratio} = \frac{\text{Income Before Income Taxes} + \text{Interest Expense} + \text{Lease Expense}}{\text{Interest Expense} + \text{Lease Expense}}$$

Activity Ratios

It is management's responsibility to provide products and services to members. Activity ratios measure the effectiveness with which management uses the resources of the club.

Inventory Turnover

This ratio measures the number of times inventory turns over during the period. Generally, the greater the number of times the better, because inventories can be expensive to maintain. Inventory turnovers are usually calculated separately for food items and beverage items. To calculate inventory turnover, it is first necessary to determine the average inventory. This is accomplished by adding inventory at the beginning and end of the period and then dividing that figure by two. The inventory turnover of a product can be calculated as follows:

$$\text{Product Inventory Turnover} = \frac{\text{Cost of Product Used}}{\text{Average Product Inventory}}$$

Property and Equipment Turnover

This ratio measures management's effectiveness in using the property and equipment. A high turnover suggests that the club's property and equipment are being used effectively to generate revenue; a low turnover suggests that the club is not making effective use of its property and equipment. The property and equipment turnover is calculated by dividing average total property and equipment into total revenue for the period. To calculate the property and equipment turnover, it is first necessary to determine the average total property and equipment. This is accomplished by totaling property and equipment at the beginning and end of the period and then dividing that figure by two. The property and equipment turnover can be calculated as follows:

$$\text{Property and Equipment Turnover} = \frac{\text{Total Revenue}}{\text{Average Total Property and Equipment}}$$

Operating Ratios

Operating ratios assist management in analyzing the operations of the club. These ratios relate expenses to revenue and are useful for control purposes when the ratio results are compared with budgeted or planned ratio goals. Significant variations between actual ratio results and budgeted or planned goals may indicate the need for further analysis and corrective action by management. The operating ratios discussed below are only a selected few of the many that management should consider. Each departmental manager should calculate the ratio to departmental revenue of:

- Cost of sales
- Major expenses
- Total expenses
- Departmental net income (loss)

Profit Margin Ratio

This ratio measures management's overall ability to produce positive results of operations as shown on the Statement of Activities by generating revenue and controlling expenses. The profit margin ratio is calculated by dividing results of operations by total revenue. The results of operations figure represents income after *all* expenses have been deducted—expenses controllable by management and expenses directly related to decisions made by the club's board of directors. The profit margin ratio can be calculated as follows:

$$\text{Profit Margin Ratio} = \frac{\text{Results of Operations}}{\text{Total Revenue}}$$

Average Food Check

This operating ratio reveals the amount of the average food check per cover and is calculated by dividing total food revenue by the number of covers. Covers refers to members and their guests served in the food operation during the period. The average food check can be calculated as follows:

$$\text{Average Food Check} = \frac{\text{Total Food Revenue}}{\text{Number of Covers}}$$

The average food check may be calculated for each food outlet and also by meal period and day of the week.

Average Room Rate

Although rates may vary within a club operating overnight rooms, managers calculate an average room rate. The average room rate reveals the average rate charged per paid room occupied and is calculated by dividing overnight rooms revenue by the number of paid rooms occupied. Paid rooms occupied are rooms occupied by club members and guests on a paid basis. The average room rate can be calculated as follows:

$$\text{Average Room Rate} = \frac{\text{Rooms Revenue}}{\text{Paid Rooms Occupied}}$$

Food Cost Percentage

This operating ratio compares the cost of food sales to food revenue. Many managers rely heavily on this ratio in determining whether food costs are reasonable. Food cost percentage is calculated by dividing the cost of food sold by food revenue. The food cost percentage can be calculated as follows:

$$\text{Food Cost Percentage} = \frac{\text{Cost of Food Sold}}{\text{Food Revenue}}$$

Labor Cost Percentage

The largest expense for virtually all clubs is labor. Labor expense includes total payroll and related expenses for all departments and operational areas of the club. A general labor cost percentage is calculated by dividing total payroll and related expenses by total revenue. This general labor cost percentage is simply a benchmark for making broad comparisons. For control purposes, labor cost percentages should be calculated and analyzed for each department and operational area of the property. The labor cost percentage can be calculated as follows:

$$\text{Labor Cost Percentage} = \frac{\text{Payroll and Related Expenses}}{\text{Total Revenue}}$$

Facility Maintenance Percentage

This operating ratio compares the total cost of maintaining the club's facilities as recorded in the facility maintenance accounts to the total revenue of the club. The calculation is as follows:

$$\text{Facility Maintenance Percentage} = \frac{\text{Facility Maintenance Expense}}{\text{Total Revenue}}$$

Golf Course Maintenance Per Hole

This operating ratio compares to cost of maintaining the golf course to the number of holes and is useful for comparison to other similar golf courses.

$$\text{Golf Course Maintenance Per Hole} = \frac{\text{Golf Course Maintenance Expense}}{\text{Number of Holes}}$$

Membership Ratios

A membership is defined as one paying account, whether or not more than one individual belongs to the account. This definition excludes all complimentary and any other non-paying members.

Membership Attrition

Membership attrition is measured on an annual basis. Since memberships are added and dropped each month, the attrition formula is best calculated using the average opening monthly membership for a rolling twelve-month period. The definitions of the attributes are as follows:

Memberships at the beginning of the period (Membership accounts)
add   New Memberships
add   Reinstated memberships that had been dropped in previous periods
deduct   Dropped memberships
Memberships at the end of the period

Note that this definition excludes all changes between paying membership categories such as regulars and seniors.

$$\text{Membership Attrition} = \frac{\text{Aggregate Dropped Memberships for 12 Months}}{\text{12-Month Average Beginning Memberships}}$$

An example is as follows:

Month	Beginning Memberships	Dropped Memberships
January	2,000	10
February	2,045	15
March	2,040	5
April	2,060	12
May	2,070	8
June	2,100	10
July	2,125	14
August	2,130	10
September	2,140	12
October	2,150	6
November	2,175	4
December	2,190	8
Total	25,225	114
Average	2,102	

$$\text{Membership Attrition} = \frac{114}{2,102}$$

$$= \underline{\underline{5.4\%}}$$

Average Initiation Fee

The average initiation fee collected is determined as follows:

$$\text{Average Initition Fee} = \frac{\text{Total Initition Fees Collected}}{\text{Total New Memberships}}$$

Average Monthly Dues

The average monthly dues collected is determined as follows:

$$\text{Average Monthly Dues} = \frac{\text{Total Monthly Dues Collected for the Period}}{\text{Total Monthly Dues-Paying Memberships for the Period}}$$

Number of Club Uses per Period

The number of club uses per period is an important statistic to use when evaluating utilization. This number is used to track peak periods and for a variety of operating decisions such as marketing and staffing. It may be calculated for each department as well as the total for the club for the period.

Appendix C
Projections and Budgeting

An effective budgeting procedure is one of the devices management has developed to project and monitor operations. Both city and country clubs need to use effective budgeting and forecasting procedures.

As in a business entity, where the directors have a responsibility to the shareholders, a club's directors are morally and legally responsible to the members for reasonable financial results. A club is an important part of members' social lives where substantial dollars are spent to provide services, recreational facilities, activities, and entertainment. Control of those expenditures concerns all parties involved. Although member satisfaction is paramount, club management is also responsible for ensuring desirable operating and financial results.

One of the ways to ensure desirable operating and financial results is through an efficient budgetary process, which encompasses planning the most effective course of action to be taken for the upcoming period, scheduling and acquiring the funds necessary to traverse that period, controlling expenditures of those funds, and appraising the results of such expenditures. Effective planning includes both long-term planning, which involves establishing the objectives of the club and forecasting the conditions that will affect these objectives, and short-term planning and budgeting, which includes planning cash flows in the short run, controlling them, and appraising the results of the operations of the club.

The budgetary process includes the following three critical components:

- Organization of the budgeting process
- Preparation of the operating, capital, and cash budgets
- Application of budgets and review of results

Organization of the Budgeting Process

Organization of the budgeting process entails establishing its procedural details. A properly organized budgeting procedure provides a defined sequence of who shall participate, when, and how.

Operating and capital budgets begin with the department heads. After department heads have assembled their budgets, often with the help of the club's controller, they meet with the club's general manager/chief operating officer to discuss and prove the numbers. At this point, it is important to identify and remove excess departmental expense to end up with a reasonable budget. The general manager/chief operating officer and the controller will combine all departmental budgets into the total club's operating budget and, once satisfied that the numbers are appropriate, will present the budget to the club's finance committee (sometimes called the budget committee), along with a recommended dues increase needed to offset the deficit, if any. This process is replicated with the capital budget using the appropriate supporting documentation for each item in the budget. The controller, working with the general manager/chief operating officer, should prepare the cash budget. Once approved by the finance committee these financial documents are to be presented to the Board for adoption.

An appropriate time schedule should be set to regulate the budgeting process. The period that a budget will cover should match the needs of the club. Budgeting is usually done on an annual basis, though it is becoming fairly common to see multi-year budgets being developed.

Budgets can be either fixed or variable, depending on the function they are to serve. A fixed budget establishes set expenditure levels for a definite time period. A fixed budget format most aptly applies to the capital budget, which includes long-term expenditures such as additions to or renovation of the clubhouse, purchases of equipment, and other major expenditures. A fixed budget format may also be appropriately applied to allocations for operating the club secretary's office (if appropriate), the membership and social committees, and the administrative office controlling the club's operating departments.

A variable budget is most suitable to activities that will incur varying levels of operating costs for different volumes of business and revenues. The food, beverage, and rooms departments (if applicable) are prime examples. A variable budget has built-in provisions for constant revisions in estimates of related income, expenses, and resulting cash flow to meet the projected budgeted result.

The club controller is expected to prepare forecasts of all financial and fixed charges such as insurance, taxes, and interest.

The chairman of the membership committee, in agreement with the general manager/chief operating officer, should submit a proposed quota of membership by classes in order to ascertain anticipated revenue from membership dues and new membership initiation and transfer fees.

The assembly of budget estimates, their digest, and the formulation of the budget plan are a direct function of the department heads under the direction of the club's general manager/chief operating officer and controller.

The budget should be formulated in two separate parts, the operating budget and the cash flow budget. No set form is required, but it should be kept simple and understandable.

A written procedure budget defining the responsibility for each section is the key to successful planning and execution. After finalizing the budget, the finance committee recommends the approval of the budget plan by the Board.

The Board of Directors or Governors is the final authority and approves the budget as submitted or amended.

The budget is a plan, not a law. It is an instruction to the several responsible operating and administrative heads as to the program to be executed and the results, in financial terms, that they are expected to produce. It provides definite objectives with regard to future operations.

At the same time, management policies for the future are formulated and clarified. The budget is a convenient yardstick for measuring efficiency of operations, both in general and in detail. It fixes the responsibility for achieving each estimated result on some individual or department and, if properly communicated, can develop good working relationships to achieve the common goal. Should the budget process extend into multi-year formats, it should be noted that each ensuing year must be periodically verified to ensure that any changes in operations, etc., are properly reflected in the later years.

Preparation of the Operating, Capital, and Cash Budgets

The club's general manager/chief operating officer is responsible for coordinating the preparation of the various budgets and for providing the appropriate information on which departments will base their operating plans. Budget preparation requires the participation of each department head. Participation is an essential ingredient for a successful budget recipe, since it serves as a way to naturally coordinate the activities of each department.

For each department, income and expenses must be forecast for the appropriate period, usually seasonally or monthly, but at least annually. Estimates of income and expenses are made by carefully weighing past performance, current trends in business, prospective higher prices and taxes, increased labor costs, and other pertinent data to determine their effect upon past, present, and future operating results.

In order for departments to accurately formulate their preliminary budgets, the club's general manager/chief operating officer should provide, with the assistance of the controller, appropriate pricing rates or strategies and inflation rates for inventories, materials, and labor.

The general manager/chief operating officer should make sure that the list of all revenue and expense estimates is complete before proceeding. The following is a checklist indicating the type of information needed for the budget:

- Changes in operating environment
- Forecast of economic conditions
- Departmental sales and other income
- Inventory costs
- Direct material costs
- Direct labor hours and costs
- Maintenance and cleaning costs
- Utility expenses
- Indirect labor and expenses such as administrative and general overhead
- Non-operating income and expenses such as leases and pro shop

Once the preliminary departmental budgets are complete, the club's general manager/chief operating officer should produce for the finance committee an estimate of the operating plan for the entire group of operating departments. This must be a technically competent plan containing the following fundamental information:

- An estimate of revenues should be made by month for each operating department with clear explanations for changes from past experience.

- Planned cost and expense ratios to sales should be disclosed representing the management's established pre-standards.

- The expected profit or loss realization is projected from the individual and total of all operating departments.

- Comparative data.

These should not be "guesstimates" but a complete, detailed projection of planned results. Club management prepares, submits, and recommends this part of the budget as the initial step toward finalizing the master budget.

Next, management should recommend capital improvement projects that are required or contemplated for the period. These should have been reviewed at the committee and department head level and prioritized by the long-range planning committee.

For changes or new equipment that can be cost-justified in savings, the cost and savings should be worked out in detail and demonstrated. For changes or equipment that can be cost-justified in added gross profits through increased sales or revenue, these increases should be illustrated. New equipment or changes that are recommended solely on the basis of improved services must be illustrated and planned on this basis. All the aforementioned should be coupled with a formal approval process prior to starting projects.

In all cases, carefully prepared estimates of the initial and continuing operating costs of each project or item of equipment should be obtained and submitted.

The next step in the budgeting program is the submission by management of expense estimates for all non-revenue departments under its control and responsibility. The basis of these estimates usually is the historical costs of prior years. Zero-based budgeting can be used in this area. Management should question if any of these expenses can be eliminated entirely. Are certain expenses incurred for the benefit of only a few members?

As a final step, management recommends projects that can reduce costs or expenses or improve efficiency. Finally, the finance committee, working with the general manager/chief operating officer, forecasts the anticipated dues revenue for the year and, if appropriate, recommends an increase in dues to balance the budget.

After preliminary budgets have been scrutinized and revised, the master budget will consist of the operating budget, the capital budget, and the cash flow budget. The master budget is then submitted to the Board of Directors or Governors for approval or revision.

The cash flow budget is an extremely important tool of financial administration because its principal purpose is to predict if, when, and by how much the club's cash flow resources will either be in excess of estimated requirements or become insufficient to cover checks that must be written during the budget period. Projection of a cash flow budget to determine what funds will be required, when they will be needed, and from what sources they will be derived is an important phase of budgeting, especially when working capital is limited.

The most common method of preparing a cash flow budget is the cash receipts and disbursements method, which consists of initially recording each and every source of cash receipt and disbursement. The usefulness of a cash flow budget depends on its accuracy, so preparation calls for careful attention to projecting the amount and timing of revenues and expenses.

One of the most critical steps in preparing a cash flow budget is an accurate forecast of receipt and sales collections, usually done by an economic or statistical forecast based on past records. First, a sales forecast is made for the amount of membership dues, the amount of food sales, etc. Then a total dollar amount is forecast for the month. Finally, an analysis is performed to determine the time lag between when receipts are due and when they are actually collected. A suitable worksheet should be used to record estimated cash receipts and disbursements. For example, accounts receivable can be scheduled as follows:

Analysis of December Accounts Receivable
(%) Percentages are based on historical payment rates

	DEC.	JAN.	FEB.	MARCH
Prior month's receivables	20,000	10,000	15,000	12,000
Current month's billings	100,000	150,000	120,000	
Total	120,000	160,000	135,000	
Estimated receipts				
100% prior month	20,000	10,000	15,000	
90% current month	90,000	135,000	108,000	
Total receipts	110,000	145,000	123,000	
Less				
Bad debts	–	–	1,000	
Net cash receipts	110,000	145,000	122,000	

When accurate records are kept, adjustments to formulas (historical payment rates) can be made when changes outdate existing projections.

Application of Budget

The budget should serve as a control or measuring stick for month-to-month operations. It is customary for the finance committee to review the actual performance of departmental results on either a quarterly or monthly basis.

In either case, the annual budget should be broken down into quarterly or monthly periods and a report should be prepared comparing the actual results with the budgeted program. Over-performance is as open to criticism as under-performance. The aim is to adhere to the objectives established.

The club controller will advise the club's general manager/chief operating officer and the treasurer of the status of the actual expenditures from time to time as compared with budget authorizations. They will report to the finance committee any excess of actual commitments or actual expenditures over authorization as soon as the information comes to their knowledge.

The club controller has no control power over expenditures, nor has the finance committee. It must be exercised through the Board by club management or officers to whom power is delegated.

After management and directors have appraised the overall operation by analyzing both positive and negative variances of actual budget performances, they are in a better position to evaluate the strengths and weaknesses of a club's operation, and are better prepared to plan and revise their strategies and policies for achieving desired financial results.

Appendix D
Sample Chart of Accounts

The following pages present a sample chart of accounts that is intended only as a guide to establishing an accounting system for recording business transactions. No attempt has been made to provide for every type of club. The chart of accounts presented here is sufficiently flexible to allow clubs to add or delete accounts to meet their needs and requirements.

Consistency is the key. Leaving room to add accounts is important when setting up a new chart of accounts. If you are transitioning to new software, look at the opportunities afforded in this area to model your accounts based on the guidelines attached. Most club accounting software allows for a set-up very similar to the format shown in this book.

The first part of an account number will indicate which revenue department or cost center is involved (if any). This sample system uses the following designations:

0	Non-Allocated
1	Food
2	Beverage
3	Entertainment
4	Overnight Rooms
5	Golf Operations
6	Golf Shop
7	Golf Course Maintenance
8	Racquet Sports
9	Racquet Shop
10	Aquatic Sports
11	Health and Fitness
12	Locker Rooms
13	Telecommunications
14	Other Operating Departments
15	Rentals
16	Administrative and General
17	Clubhouse
18	Energy
19	Facility Maintenance
20	Fixed Charges

The departmental prefix is then followed by a three or four digit number indicating the sub-account classification. This sample chart of accounts uses the following three-digit assignments:

100–199	Assets
200–299	Liabilities
300–399	Net Assets (Members' Equity)
400–499	Revenues
500–599	Cost of Sales
600–699	Payroll and Payroll Related
700–799	Operating Expenses
800–849	Decorations and Entertainment
850–899	Energy and Facility Maintenance
900–999	Fixed Charges

For example, the account numbers for dues and subscriptions (sub-account 750) for the food, beverage, and overnight rooms would be as follows:

1-750	Food Dues and Subscriptions
2-750	Beverage Dues and Subscriptions
4-750	Overnight Rooms Dues and Subscriptions

The following pages present a more detailed assignment of the major sub-account numbers. To facilitate use, the sample chart of accounts is presented in two formats. A numerical presentation is followed by an alphabetical presentation by major category.

ASSETS

Cash and cash equivalents

100	Cash—house
102	Cash—checking
103	Cash—payroll
104	Cash—savings
106	Cash—other
110	Certificates of deposit
112	Money market funds

Short-term investments

115	Investments—short-term

Receivables

120	Accounts receivable—members
122	Accounts receivable—other clubs
124	Notes receivable
126	Deferred initiation fees
128	Other receivables (employee)
129	Allowance for doubtful accounts

Inventories

130	Inventory—food
132	Inventory—liquor
133	Inventory—wine and beer

135	Inventory—sundry
136	Inventory—merchandise

Prepaid expenses

140	Prepaid insurance—general
141	Prepaid insurance—workers' compensation
142	Prepaid insurance—medical
143	Prepaid insurance—other
144	Prepaid rent
145	Property taxes paid in advance
146	Prepaid—other
147	Prepaid china, glassware, and silver

Other current assets

148	Transfers and exchange
149	Other current assets

Noncurrent receivables

150	Loans receivable—noncurrent
152	Notes receivable—noncurrent
155	Interest receivable—noncurrent

Property and equipment

160	Land
161	Construction/work in progress
162	Leasehold and leasehold improvements
163	Building and building improvements
164	Golf course improvements
165	Equipment
166	Furniture and fixtures
167	Technology and telecommunications
168	Capital leases
169	China, glassware, silver, linen, and uniforms

Accumulated depreciation and amortization

170	Accumulated amortization—leasehold and leasehold improvements
172	Accumulated depreciation—building and building improvements
174	Accumulated depreciation—golf course improvements
175	Accumulated depreciation—equipment
176	Accumulated depreciation—furniture and fixtures
177	Accumulated depreciation—technology and telecommunications
178	Accumulated depreciation—capital leases
179	Accumulated depreciation—china, glassware, silver, linen, and uniforms

Other assets

180	Security deposits

182	Deferred charges
184	Cash surrender value—life insurance
186	Closing costs (amortize)
188	Other noncurrent assets

LIABILITIES

Payables

200	Notes payable—short-term
202	Accounts payable
205	Intercompany
206	Payables—other

Taxes payable and accrued

210	OASDI/MEDIC withheld
212	Federal income tax withheld
213	State income tax withheld
214	Local taxes withheld
215	Withholdings—other
220	Federal unemployment tax payable
222	State unemployment tax payable
223	Property tax payable
224	Sales and use tax payable
225	Occupancy tax payable
226	Federal income tax payable
227	State income tax payable
228	Taxes payable—other

Voluntary deductions

230	Employee deduction—medical
232	Employee deduction—dental
233	Employee deduction—life insurance
234	Employee deduction—garnishment
235	Employee salary deferral plan
236	Employee deduction—other

Accrued expenses

240	Accrued compensation
242	Accrued vacation pay
245	Accrued operating expenses
246	Accrued capital expenditures
248	Accrued other

Long-term debt (current portion)

250	Loans payable—current
252	Notes payable—current
254	Utility assessments—current
256	Obligations under capital lease—current

Deferred revenues

260	Deferred initiation fees
262	Deferred membership dues
264	Deferred capital charges
266	Deferred special assessments
268	Deferred program revenues
269	Deferred special event revenues
270	Deferred income taxes—current

Special purpose funds

271	Golf activity funds
272	Grounds activity funds
273	House activity funds
274	Racquet activity funds
275	Other special purpose funds

Other current liabilities

280	Due to golf professional
281	Due to racquets professional
282	Due to other professional

Long-term debt

285	Certificates/bonds payable—long-term
286	Secured loans—long-term
288	Utility assessments—long-term
290	Notes payable—long-term
292	Mortgage payable—long-term
294	Obligation under capital lease—long-term
296	Long-term debt—other

Other long-term liabilities

298	Deferred income taxes—noncurrent
299	Obligations to members—noncurrent

NET ASSETS (MEMBERS' EQUITY)

300	Capital stock/membership certificates
310	Paid-in capital
320	Treasury stock/certificates
330	Unrealized gain (loss) on marketable securities
350	Designated assets
360	Undesignated assets
399	Income summary

REVENUES

Non-allocated revenues

400	Membership dues

401	Initiation fees
402	Capital charges
403	Special assessments
404	Unused food/other minimums
405	Service charge
406	Rentals
407	Interest income
408	Investment income
409	Other revenues

Food

410–419	Food—à la carte
420–429	Food—club event
430–439	Food—banquet
440–449	Food—snack bars
450–459	Food—tournaments
460–469	Unused minimum
470–479	Dining room rentals
480–489	Service charge
490–499	Food—other

Beverage

410–419	Beverage—à la carte
420–429	Beverage—club event
430–439	Beverage—banquet
440–449	Beverage—snack bars
450–459	Beverage—tournaments
480–489	Service charge
490–499	Beverage—other

Entertainment

410–419	Entertainment—house
420–429	Entertainment—club event
430–439	Entertainment—banquet
450–459	Entertainment—special event
490–499	Entertainment—other

Overnight rooms

410–419	Rooms—transient—guest
420–429	Rooms—transient—member
430–439	Rooms—permanent
460–469	Miscellaneous
490–499	Overnight rooms other

Golf operations

410–419	Golf guest fees
420–424	Golf cart fees
425–429	Golf fees—other

430–439	Club storage and repair
440–449	Golf clinics and lessons
450–459	Golf tournaments
460–469	Golf miscellaneous
490-499	Golf other

Golf shop

410–419	Golf shop club (equipment)
420–429	Golf shop accessories
430–439	Golf shop apparel
440–449	Golf shop logo merchandise
450–459	Golf shop novelties
460–460	Golf shop miscellaneous
490–499	Golf shop other

Racquet sports

410–419	Racquet guest fees
420–429	Racquet activity/program fees
430–439	Racquet rentals
440–449	Racquet clinics and lessons
450–459	Racquet tournaments
460–469	Racquet sports miscellaneous
490–499	Racquet sports other

Racquet shop

410–419	Racquet shop equipment
420–429	Racquet shop accessories
430–439	Racquet shop apparel
440–449	Racquet shop logo merchandise
450–459	Racquet shop novelties
460–469	Racquet shop miscellaneous
490–499	Racquet shop other

Aquatic sports

410–419	Aquatic guest fees
420–429	Aquatic activity/program fees
430–439	Aquatic rentals
440–449	Aquatic clinics and lessons
450–459	Aquatic tournaments
460–469	Aquatic miscellaneous
470–479	Aquatic towel fees
490–499	Aquatic sports other

Health and fitness

410–419	Health and fitness guest fees
420–429	Health and fitness activity/program fees
430–439	Health and fitness training
440–449	Health and fitness miscellaneous

450–459	Health and fitness locker rentals
460–469	Health and fitness merchandise sales
470–479	Health and fitness towel fees
490–499	Health and fitness other

Locker rooms

410–419	Locker rental—guests
420–429	Locker rental—members
430–439	Locker rental—tournaments/outings
440–449	Locker rooms shoe fees
470–479	Locker rooms towel fees
490–499	Locker rooms other

Telecommunications

410–419	Call accounting
420–429	Internet access
430–439	Video revenue
440–449	Equipment rental
460–469	Miscellaneous
490–499	Other

Other operating departments

410–419	Guest fees
420–429	Activity/program fees
430–439	Rentals
440–449	Club events
450–459	Tournaments
460–469	Miscellaneous
490–499	Other

Rentals and other revenue

410–419	Space rental
420–429	Concession
430–439	Cash discounts earned
440–449	Interest income
450–459	Commissions
460–469	Miscellaneous
490–499	Other

COST OF SALES

Food

510	Dining room supplies—inventoried
551	Co-op purchases
552	Food purchases—vendors
553	Less: Cost of meals provided to employees
554	Less: Credit for gratis food

555	Trade discounts
558	Transfers between Food and Beverage

Beverage

510	Bar supplies—inventoried
551	Beer purchases
552	Less: bottle deposit refunds
553	Liquor purchases
554	Wine purchases
555	Non-alcoholic purchases
556	Less: credit for gratis beverage
557	Trade discounts
558	Transfers between Food and Beverage

Golf shop

530	Cost of merchandise sold—golf shop

Racquet shop

530	Cost of merchandise sold—racquet shop

Health and fitness

530	Cost of merchandise sold—health and fitness

PAYROLL AND RELATED EXPENSES

600	Management and supervisory
610	Payroll full time—regular
611	Payroll full time—overtime
612	Payroll full time—holiday
613	Payroll full time—vacation
614	Payroll full time—sick
620	Payroll seasonal—regular
621	Payroll seasonal—overtime
622	Payroll seasonal—holiday
623	Payroll seasonal—vacation
624	Payroll seasonal—sick
650	Leased employees
660	Federal unemployment expense
661	MEDIC expense
662	OASDI expense
663	Other local tax expense
664	State unemployment tax expense
670	Defined benefit plans
671	Dental insurance
672	Disability insurance
673	Health insurance
674	Life insurance
675	Employee meals

| 680 | Workers' compensation insurance |
| 690 | Other |

Given the importance of food revenue and food payroll to most clubs, a club may wish to break its food payroll into greater detail than it does for other departments. The following Food accounts demonstrate this approach.

Food

630	Kitchen payroll—regular
631	Kitchen payroll—overtime
632	Kitchen payroll—holiday
633	Kitchen payroll—vacation
634	Kitchen payroll—sick
635	Snack bar—regular
636	Snack bar—overtime
637	Snack bar—holiday
638	Snack bar—vacation
639	Snack bar—sick
640	Waitstaff payroll—regular
641	Waitstaff payroll—overtime
642	Waitstaff payroll—holiday
643	Waitstaff payroll—vacation
644	Waitstaff payroll—sick

OPERATING EXPENSES

700	Athletic supplies
701	Cleaning supplies
702	Dry cleaning supplies
703	Equipment rental
704	Equipment repair and maintenance
705	General supplies—other
706	Gratis beverage
707	Gratis food
708	Guest supplies
709	Laundry supplies
710	Member supplies
711	Paper supplies
712	Spoiled or damaged goods
713	Towels and amenities
714	Utensils
715	China
716	Glassware
717	Linens
718	Silver
720	Contract services
725	Equipment lease

726	Mechanical lease
727	Vehicle lease
728	Credit card fees
729	Equipment expense (A&G)
730	Club publications
731	Committee supplies
732	Library
733	Menus
734	Newspapers and periodicals
735	Office supplies
736	Postage
737	Printing and copying
738	Stationery
739	Telephone
740	Contract maintenance—hardware
741	Contract maintenance—software
742	Computer lease
743	Data processing supplies
744	Software expenses
745	Computer expenses—other
750	Dues and subscriptions
751	Employee handbook
752	Employee housing
753	Professional development
754	Recruitment
755	Relocation
756	Training and education
757	Transportation
758	Travel and entertainment
759	Uniforms
760	Commissions
761	Credit and collections
762	Directors and committees
763	Donations
764	Licenses and permits
765	Professional fees
766	Provision for doubtful accounts
767	Loss and damages
768	Trade association and conferences
769	Website
770	Applicants
771	Cart batteries and maintenance
772	Cart rental
773	Court maintenance
774	Drainage repair and maintenance
775	Driving range

776	Fences and bridges repair and maintenance
777	Fertilizers
778	Fuel
779	Gasoline and lubricants
780	Golf course equipment repair and maintenance
781	Irrigation repairs and maintenance
782	Landscaping—department use
783	Prizes
784	Refuse removal—department use
785	Roads and path maintenance
786	Sand, gravel, topdressing
787	Seeds, flowers, shrubs
788	Small tools
789	Topsoil
790	Tournament expenses
791	Tree care
792	Utilities—department use
793	Vehicle expenses
794	Chemicals—aquatic sports
795	Advertising and promotion
796	Marketing
797	Miscellaneous
798	Security

DECORATIONS AND ENTERTAINMENT

800	Decorations and flowers
801	Decorating services
802	Displays
803	Fixtures (non asset)
804	Artwork—leased
805	Engraving and lettering
806	Plants and plant care
807	Trophies
830	Advertising and promotion
831	Agency fees—entertainment
832	Committee expenses
833	Contract entertainment
834	Equipment rental—entertainment
835	Films
836	Live bands
837	Taped music
838	Digital music
839	Cable TV
840	Children's books and toys
841	Prizes and favors

842	Royalties
843	Special event entertainment
844	Other entertainment
845	Satellite TV

ENERGY AND FACILITY MAINTENANCE

850	Clubhouse—electricity
851	Electricity—other
852	Streets—electricity
855	Heating oil
856	Natural gas
857	Propane
858	Steam
860	Water—main
861	Water—pump stations
862	Water hydrants
863	Water—sports departments
864	Energy costs—sports departments
870	Building repair and maintenance
871	Building supplies
872	Contract maintenance—equipment
873	Contract maintenance—mechanical
874	Curtains and draperies
875	Elevators
876	Engineering
877	Floor coverings
878	Furniture repair and maintenance
879	Grounds and landscaping
880	HVAC
881	Painting
882	Pest control
883	Plowing
884	Plumbing
885	Refuse removal
886	Electrical and mechanical equipment

FIXED CHARGES

900	Management fees
910	Buildings
911	Land
914	Other
919	Telecommunications
920	Auto

921	Building and contents
922	Directors and officers
923	Fiduciary
924	Key man
925	Liability
926	Oil tank
927	Other
928	Pesticide
929	Umbrella
930	Business
931	Other
932	Personal property
933	Real estate
934	Use
935	Utility
940	Current federal income tax
941	Current state income tax
942	Deferred federal income tax
943	Deferred state income tax
950	Interest on mortgage payable
951	Interest on notes payable
952	Interest—obligation under capital lease
953	Interest—other long-term debt
954	Interest—other
960	Amortization—capital leases
961	Depreciation—building improvements
962	Depreciation—equipment
963	Depreciation—furniture and fixtures
964	Depreciation—golf course improvements
965	Depreciation—technology and telecommunications
966	Depreciation—building
970	Fixed charges—other

Alternate Presentation:
Alphabetical by Major Category

Note: for clarification, this presentation will in some cases prefix the account number with the department number. In cases where various departments would use the same account, the department is shown as *v* for *various*. In the revenues section, where a revenue account could be one of a range of numbers, only the first number of the range is listed. For example, Golf Guest Fees, which can be broken into various accounts in the range of 410–419, is shown as 4-410.

STATEMENT OF FINANCIAL POSITION

120	Accounts receivable—members
122	Accounts receivable—other clubs
202	Accounts payable
246	Accrued capital expenditures
240	Accrued compensation
245	Accrued operating expenses
248	Accrued other
242	Accrued vacation pay
170	Accumulated amortization—leasehold and leasehold improvements
172	Accumulated depreciation—building and building improvements
178	Accumulated depreciation—capital leases
179	Accumulated depreciation—china, glassware, silver, linen and uniforms
175	Accumulated depreciation—equipment
176	Accumulated depreciation—furniture and fixtures
174	Accumulated depreciation—golf course improvements
177	Accumulated depreciation—technology and telecommunications
129	Allowance for doubtful accounts
163	Building and building improvements
168	Capital leases
300	Capital stock/membership certificates
102	Cash—checking
100	Cash—house
103	Cash—payroll
106	Cash—other
104	Cash—savings
184	Cash surrender value—life insurance
110	Certificates of deposit
285	Certificates/bonds payable—long term
169	China, glassware, silver, linen, and uniforms
186	Closing costs (amortize)
161	Construction/work in progress
264	Deferred capital charges
182	Deferred charges
270	Deferred income taxes—current
298	Deferred income taxes—noncurrent
126	Deferred initiation fees (asset)
260	Deferred initiation fees (liability)
262	Deferred membership dues
268	Deferred program revenues
266	Deferred special assessments
269	Deferred special event revenues

350	Designated assets
280	Due to golf professional
282	Due to other professional
281	Due to racquets professional
236	Employee deduction—other
232	Employee deduction—dental
234	Employee deduction—garnishment
233	Employee deduction—life insurance
230	Employee deduction—medical
235	Employee salary deferral plan
165	Equipment
226	Federal income tax payable
212	Federal income tax withheld
220	Federal unemployment tax payable
166	Furniture and fixtures
271	Golf activity funds
164	Golf course improvements
272	Grounds activity funds
273	House activity funds
399	Income summary
205	Intercompany (payable)
155	Interest receivable—noncurrent
130	Inventory—food
132	Inventory—liquor
136	Inventory—merchandise
135	Inventory—sundry
133	Inventory—wine and beer
115	Investments—short term
160	Land
162	Leasehold and leasehold improvements
250	Loans payable—current
150	Loans receivable—noncurrent
214	Local taxes withheld
296	Long-term debt—other
112	Money market funds
292	Mortgage payable—long-term
200	Notes payable—short-term
252	Notes payable—current
290	Notes payable—long-term
124	Notes receivable
152	Notes receivable—noncurrent
210	OASDI/MEDIC withheld
294	Obligation under capital lease—long-term
299	Obligations to members—noncurrent
256	Obligations under capital lease—current
225	Occupancy tax payable

149	Other current assets
188	Other noncurrent assets
128	Other receivables (employee)
275	Other special purpose funds
310	Paid-in capital
206	Payables—other
146	Prepaid—other
147	Prepaid china, glassware, and silver
140	Prepaid insurance—general
142	Prepaid insurance—medical
143	Prepaid insurance—other
141	Prepaid insurance—workers' compensation
144	Prepaid rent
223	Property tax payable
145	Property taxes paid in advance
274	Racquet activity funds
224	Sales and use tax payable
286	Secured loans—long-term
180	Security deposits
227	State income tax payable
213	State income tax withheld
222	State unemployment tax payable
228	Taxes payable—other
167	Technology and telecommunications
148	Transfers and exchange
320	Treasury stock/certificates
360	Undesignated assets
330	Unrealized gain (loss) on marketable securities
254	Utility assessments—current
288	Utility assessments—long-term
215	Withholdings—other

REVENUES

14-420	Activity/program fees—other
10-420	Aquatic activity/program fees
10-410	Aquatic guest fees
10-440	Aquatic clinics and lessons
10-460	Aquatic miscellaneous
10-490	Aquatic other
10-430	Aquatic rentals
10-450	Aquatic tournaments
10-470	Aquatic towel fees
2-410	Beverage—à la carte
2-430	Beverage—banquet
2-420	Beverage—club event

2-440	Beverage—snack bars
2-450	Beverage—tournaments
2-490	Beverage—other
13-410	Call accounting revenues
0-402	Capital charges
15-430	Cash discounts earned
14-440	Club events—other
15-450	Commissions
15-420	Concession revenue
3-430	Entertainment—banquet
3-420	Entertainment—club event
3-410	Entertainment—house
3-490	Entertainment—other
3-450	Entertainment—special event
13-440	Equipment rental revenue (telecommunications)
1-410	Food—à la carte
1-430	Food—banquet
1-420	Food—club event
1-490	Food—other
1-440	Food—snack bars
1-450	Food—tournaments
5-420	Golf cart fees
5-440	Golf clinics and lessons
5-430	Golf club storage and repair
5-425	Golf fees—other
5-410	Golf guest fees
5-460	Golf miscellaneous
5-490	Golf other
6-420	Golf shop accessories
6-430	Golf shop apparel
6-410	Golf shop club (equipment)
6-440	Golf shop logo merchandise
6-460	Golf shop miscellaneous
6-450	Golf shop novelties
6-490	Golf shop other
5-450	Golf tournaments
14-410	Guest fees—other
11-420	Health and fitness activity/program fees
11-410	Health and fitness guest fees
11-450	Health and fitness locker rentals
11-460	Health and fitness merchandise sales
11-440	Health and fitness miscellaneous
11-490	Health and fitness other
11-470	Health and fitness towel fees
11-430	Health and fitness training
0-401	Initiation fees

15-440	Interest income—other operating department
0-407	Interest income
13-420	Internet access revenues
0-408	Investment income
12-410	Locker rental—guests
12-420	Locker rental—members
12-430	Locker rental—tournaments/outings
12-490	Locker rooms—other
12-440	Locker rooms—shoe fees
12-470	Locker rooms—towel fees
1-470	Dining room rentals
0-400	Membership dues
14-460	Miscellaneous—other
15-460	Miscellaneous—rental revenue
14-490	Other operating department—other revenue
15-490	Other—rental revenue
0-409	Other revenues
4-430	Overnight rooms—permanent
4-460	Overnight rooms—miscellaneous
4-490	Overnight rooms—other
4-410	Overnight rooms—transient—guest
4-420	Overnight rooms—transient—member
8-420	Racquet activity/program fees
8-440	Racquet clinics and lessons
8-410	Racquet guest fees
8-460	Racquet miscellaneous
8-490	Racquet other
8-430	Racquet rentals
9-420	Racquet shop accessories
9-430	Racquet shop apparel
9-410	Racquet shop equipment
9-440	Racquet shop logo merchandise
9-460	Racquet shop miscellaneous
9-450	Racquet shop novelties
9-490	Racquet shop other
8-450	Racquet tournaments
0-406	Rentals
14-430	Rentals—other operating department
15-490	Rentals—other revenue
2-480	Service charge—beverage
1-480	Service charge—food
0-405	Service charge (non-allocated)
15-410	Space rental revenue
0-403	Special assessments
13-460	Telecommunications—miscellaneous
13-490	Telecommunications—other

14-450	Tournaments—other
0-404	Unused food/other minimums—non-allocated
1-460	Unused minimum—food (if allocated)
13-430	Video revenue

COST OF SALES

2-510	Bar supplies—inventoried
2-551	Beer purchases
1-551	Co-op purchases—food
11-530	Cost of merchandise sold—health and fitness
9-530	Cost of merchandise sold—racquet shop
6-530	Cost of merchandise sold—golf shop
1-510	Dining room supplies—inventoried
1-552	Food purchases—vendors
2-552	Less: bottle deposit refunds
1-553	Less: cost of meals provided to employees
2-556	Less: credit for gratis beverage
1-554	Less: credit for gratis food
2-553	Liquor purchases
2-555	Non-alcoholic purchases
2-557	Trade discounts—beverage
1-555	Trade discounts—food
v-558	Transfers between Food and Beverage
2-554	Wine purchases

PAYROLL AND RELATED EXPENSES

v-670	Defined benefit plans
v-671	Dental insurance
v-672	Disability insurance
v-675	Employee meals
v-660	Federal unemployment expense
v-673	Health insurance
1-632	Kitchen payroll—holiday
1-631	Kitchen payroll—overtime
1-630	Kitchen payroll—regular
1-634	Kitchen payroll—sick
1-633	Kitchen payroll—vacation
v-650	Leased employees
v-674	Life insurance
v-600	Management and supervisory
v-661	MEDIC expense
v-662	OASDI expense
v-690	Other
v-663	Other local tax expense

v-612	Payroll full-time—holiday
v-611	Payroll full-time—overtime
v-610	Payroll full-time—regular
v-614	Payroll full-time—sick
v-613	Payroll full-time—vacation
v-622	Payroll seasonal—holiday
v-621	Payroll seasonal—overtime
v-620	Payroll seasonal—regular
v-624	Payroll seasonal—sick
v-623	Payroll seasonal—vacation
1-637	Snack bar—holiday
1-636	Snack bar—overtime
1-635	Snack bar—regular
1-639	Snack bar—sick
1-638	Snack bar—vacation
v-664	State unemployment tax expense
1-642	Waitstaff payroll—holiday
1-641	Waitstaff payroll—overtime
1-640	Waitstaff payroll—regular
1-644	Waitstaff payroll—sick
1-643	Waitstaff payroll—vacation
v-680	Workers' compensation insurance

OPERATING EXPENSES

795	Advertising and promotion
770	Applicants
700	Athletic supplies
771	Cart batteries and maintenance
772	Cart rental
794	Chemicals—aquatic sports
715	China
701	Cleaning supplies
730	Club publications
760	Commissions
731	Committee supplies
745	Computer expenses—other
742	Computer lease
740	Contract maintenance—hardware
741	Contract maintenance—software
720	Contract services
773	Court maintenance
761	Credit and collections
728	Credit card fees
743	Data processing supplies
762	Directors and committees

763	Donations
774	Drainage repair and maintenance
775	Driving range
702	Dry cleaning supplies
750	Dues and subscriptions
751	Employee handbook
752	Employee housing
725	Equipment lease
703	Equipment rental
704	Equipment repair and maintenance
729	Equipment expense (A&G)
776	Fences and bridges repair and maintenance
777	Fertilizers
778	Fuel
779	Gasoline and lubricants
705	General supplies—other
716	Glassware
780	Golf course equipment repairs and maintenance
707	Gratis food
706	Gratis beverage
708	Guest supplies
781	Irrigation repairs and maintenance
782	Landscaping—department use
709	Laundry supplies
732	Library
764	Licenses and permits
717	Linens
767	Loss and damages
796	Marketing
726	Mechanical lease
710	Member supplies
733	Menus
797	Miscellaneous
734	Newspapers and periodicals
735	Office supplies
711	Paper supplies
736	Postage
737	Printing and copying
783	Prizes
753	Professional development
765	Professional fees
766	Provision for doubtful accounts
754	Recruitment
784	Refuse removal—department use
755	Relocation
785	Roads and path maintenance

786	Sand, gravel, topdressing
798	Security
787	Seeds, flowers, shrubs
718	Silver
788	Small tools
744	Software expenses
712	Spoiled or damaged goods
738	Stationery
739	Telephone
789	Topsoil
790	Tournament expenses
713	Towels and amenities
768	Trade association and conferences
756	Training and education
757	Transportation
758	Travel and entertainment
791	Tree care
759	Uniforms
714	Utensils
792	Utilities—department use
793	Vehicle expenses
727	Vehicle lease
769	Website

DECORATIONS AND ENTERTAINMENT

830	Advertising and promotion
831	Agency fees—entertainment
804	Artwork—leased
839	Cable TV
840	Children's books and toys
832	Committee expenses
833	Contract entertainment
801	Decorating services
800	Decorations and flowers
838	Digital music
802	Displays
805	Engraving and lettering
834	Equipment rental—entertainment
835	Films
803	Fixtures (non asset)
836	Live bands
844	Other entertainment
806	Plants and plant care
841	Prizes and favors
842	Royalties

845	Satellite TV
843	Special event entertainment
837	Taped music
807	Trophies

ENERGY AND FACILITY MAINTENANCE

870	Building repairs and maintenance
871	Building supplies
850	Clubhouse—electricity
872	Contract maintenance—equipment
873	Contract maintenance—mechanical
874	Curtains and draperies
886	Electrical and mechanical equipment
851	Electricity—other
875	Elevators
864	Energy costs—sports departments
876	Engineering
877	Floor coverings
878	Furniture repairs and maintenance
879	Grounds and landscaping
855	Heating oil
880	HVAC
856	Natural gas
881	Painting
882	Pest control
883	Plowing
884	Plumbing
857	Propane
885	Refuse removal
858	Steam
852	Streets—electricity
860	Water—main
861	Water—pump stations
863	Water—sports departments
862	Water hydrants

FIXED CHARGES

960	Amortization—capital leases
920	Auto insurance
921	Building and contents insurance
910	Building rent
930	Business taxes
940	Current federal income tax

941	Current state income tax
922	Directors and officers insurance
942	Deferred federal income tax
943	Deferred state income tax
966	Depreciation—building
961	Depreciation—building improvements
962	Depreciation—equipment
963	Depreciation—furniture and fixtures
964	Depreciation—golf course improvements
965	Depreciation—technology and telecommunications
923	Fiduciary insurance
970	Fixed charges—other
954	Interest—other
950	Interest on mortgage payable
951	Interest on notes payable
953	Interest—other long-term debt
952	Interest—obligation under capital lease
924	Key man insurance
911	Land rent
925	Liability insurance
900	Management fees
926	Oil tank insurance
927	Other general insurance
931	Other operating taxes
914	Other rent
932	Personal property taxes
928	Pesticide insurance
933	Real estate taxes
919	Telecommunications rent
929	Umbrella insurance
934	Use taxes
935	Utility taxes

Appendix E
Illustrated Statements and Schedules

A new feature with this edition of the *Uniform System of Financial Reporting for Clubs* is the inclusion of a historical working trial balance integrated into the preparation of the illustrated financial statements. The user will be able to follow detailed general ledger financial data as it is used to create the financial statement presentation.

The financial statement presentation in this illustration makes no effort to use every departmental supporting schedule or to use every line item on any of the schedules that are used. Its purpose is merely to show an example in sufficient detail to help users to understand the uniform system in application.

USFRC COUNTRY CLUB
TRIAL BALANCE
YEARS ENDED DECEMBER 31, 20X2 AND 20X1

TRIAL BALANCE

DESCRIPTION	20X2	20X1
Cash—house	11,000	11,000
Cash—checking	17,350	63,000
Cash—savings	45,500	635,000
Cash—other	100,000	100,000
Certificates of deposit	150,000	100,000
Money market funds	30,000	30,000
Investment—other	20,000	20,000
Accounts receivable—members	187,600	162,000
Notes receivable	—	—
Employee advances	3,500	3,200
Accounts receivable—other clubs	5,000	5,000
Receivables—other	1,000	1,000
Allowance for doubtful accounts	(3,000)	(4,000)
Inventory—food	40,000	38,000
Inventory—bar	39,500	37,900
Inventory—golf shop	8,500	18,750
Inventory—racquet shop	7,500	7,700
Inventory—aquatic shop	2,500	2,350
Inventory—other	1,500	1,700
Prepaid insurance—liability	32,000	31,500
Prepaid insurance—workers' comp	40,000	38,500
Prepaid insurance—medical	3,800	3,700
Prepaid insurance—other	750	750
Prepaid—other	—	—
Total current assets	1,454,000	1,307,050
Land	1,000,000	1,000,000
Construction/work in progress	—	25,000
Building and building improvements	3,405,000	3,275,000
Golf course improvements	4,550,000	4,400,000
Golf course equipment	875,000	822,500

	20X2	20X1	CHANGE
Cash and cash equivalents	1,053,850	939,000	114,850
Short-term investments	20,000	20,000	—
Accounts receivable—members	187,600	162,000	25,600
Other receivables	9,500	9,200	300
Less allowance for doubtful accounts	(3,000)	(4,000)	1,000
Inventories	109,500	106,400	3,100
Prepaid expenses	76,550	74,450	2,100
Total current assets	1,454,000	1,307,050	146,950

USFRC COUNTRY CLUB
TRIAL BALANCE
YEARS ENDED DECEMBER 31, 20X2 AND 20X1

Account	20X2	20X1	Total 20X2	Total 20X1	Change	Group
Furniture and fixtures	1,100,000	1,082,000				
Technology and telecommunications	185,000	165,000				
China, glassware, silver, linen, and uniforms	31,000	31,000	11,146,000	10,800,500	345,500	Property and equipment
Accumulated amortization—leasehold and leasehold improvements	(850,000)	—				
Accumulated depreciation—building and building improvements	(775,000)	(765,000)				
Accumulated depreciation—golf course improvements	(650,000)	(615,150)				
Accumulated depreciation—golf course equipment	(725,000)	(528,000)				
Accumulated depreciation—furniture and fixtures	(115,000)	(573,000)				
Accumulated depreciation—technology and telecommunications	—	(78,000)				
Accumulated depreciation—capital leases	(31,000)	—				
Accum depreciation—china, glassware, silver, linen, and uniforms	—	(31,000)	(3,146,000)	(2,590,150)	(555,850)	Accumulated depreciation
Loan closing costs	35,000	40,000				
Security deposits	5,500	5,500				
Deferred charges	—	—				
Cash surrender value—life insurance	3,200	3,000				
Other noncurrent assets	—	—	43,700	48,500	(4,800)	Other assets
Total assets			9,497,700	9,565,900	(68,200)	Total assets
			—	—	—	
Notes payable (current portion)	95,000	100,000	95,000	100,000	(5,000)	Notes payable
Accounts payable	165,000	178,000				
Intercompany payables	—	—				
Payables—other	5,000	5,000				
Employee deduction—medical	785	935				
Employee deduction—dental	365	255				
Employee deduction—life insurance	415	420				

USFRC COUNTRY CLUB
TRIAL BALANCE
YEARS ENDED DECEMBER 31, 20X2 AND 20X1

Account	20X2	20X1	20X2 Total	20X1 Total	Change	Classification
Employee deduction—garnish	350	750				
Due to golf professional	3,500	3,330				
Due to racquets professional	1,450	1,375				
Due to other professional			176,865	190,065	(13,200)	Accounts payable
OASDI/MEDIC withheld	3,000	3,500				
Federal income tax withheld	15,000	16,000				
State income tax withheld	4,000	4,500				
Local taxes withheld	2,500	2,250				
Federal unemployment tax payable	740	725				
State unemployment tax payable	740	725				
Property tax payable	115,000	113,500				
Sales and use tax payable	38,000	36,500				
Federal income tax payable	2,400	2,200				
State income tax payable	1,100	985				
Taxes payable—other			182,480	180,885	1,595	Taxes payable and accrued
Accrued compensation	20,000	22,300				
Accrued vacation pay	25,000	22,000				
Accrued other			45,000	44,300	700	Accrued expenses
Loans payable—current			75,000	75,000	–	Current portion of long-term debt
Deferred membership dues	585,000	555,000				
Deferred locker rentals	17,000	15,000				
Deferred program revenues	–	100,000				
Deferred special event revenues			602,000	670,000	(68,000)	Deferred revenue
	1,176,345	1,260,250	1,176,345	1,260,250	(83,905)	
Notes payable, net of current maturity			–	95,000	(95,000)	Notes payable, net of current maturity
Obligations under capital lease—current			50,000	75,000	(25,000)	Obligations under capital lease—current
Mortgage payable, net of current maturity			450,000	500,000	(50,000)	Mortgage payable, net of current maturity
	500,000	670,000	500,000	670,000	(170,000)	
	1,676,345	1,930,250	1,676,345	1,930,250	101,800	
Capital stock (membership certificates)	3,000,000	3,000,000	3,000,000	3,000,000	–	

USFRC COUNTRY CLUB
TRIAL BALANCE
YEARS ENDED DECEMBER 31, 20X2 AND 20X1

Capital stock (membership certificates) sold	1,300,000	1,250,000	1,300,000	1,250,000	50,000	Capital stock (membership certificates) sold
Capital stock (membership certificates) redeemed	(1,300,000)	(1,250,000)	(1,300,000)	(1,250,000)	(50,000)	Capital stock (membership certificates) redeemed
Accumulated (retained) earnings designated	505,000	400,000	505,000	400,000	105,000	Designated for capital improvements
Accumulated (retained) earnings undesignated	4,130,650	4,235,650	4,316,355	4,235,650	80,705	Undesignated
Income summary	185,705	–	185,705	–	185,705	
	7,821,355	7,635,650	7,821,355	7,635,650	185,705	
	9,497,700	9,565,900	9,497,700	9,565,900	(68,200)	
OTHER ACTIVITIES						
Membership dues	2,805,000	2,550,000	2,805,000	2,550,000		
Initiation fees	140,000	130,000	140,000	130,000		
Capital assessment	105,000	–	105,000	–		
Service charge undistributed	16,500	17,325	16,500	17,325		Service charge (17% of sales alloc to f & b)
Interest income on board designated	5,500	10,000	5,500	10,000		Capital interest income
FOOD						
Unused food minimum	7,500	7,250	7,500	7,250		Unused minimum
Food—a la carte	1,050,000	1,035,000				
Food—club event	65,000	63,500				
Food—banquet	220,000	225,000				
Food—snack bars	82,000	79,000				
Food—tournaments			1,417,000	1,402,500		Food sales
Meeting room rentals	8,350	6,950	8,350	6,950		Dining room rental
Food—other						
Total food revenue	1,432,850	1,416,700	1,432,850	1,416,700		
Co-op purchases	98,500	100,470				
Food purchases—vendors	560,000	577,705				
Food purchases—other	73,325	69,155				
Trade discounts—food			731,825	747,330		Cost of food consumed
Cost of meals provided to employees	(55,400)	(54,110)	(55,400)	(54,110)		Less credit for employees' meals
Cost of gratis food	(13,170)	(20,175)	(13,170)	(20,175)		Less credit for gratis food
Total cost of sales	663,255	673,045	663,255	673,045		
Payroll—management and supervisors	77,250	75,000				

USFRC COUNTRY CLUB
TRIAL BALANCE
YEARS ENDED DECEMBER 31, 20X2 AND 20X1

Account	20X2	20X1	20X2	20X1	Report Groupings	
Payroll full time—regular	455,000	453,500				
Payroll full time—overtime	35,000	33,250				
Payroll full time—holiday	25,000	24,100				
Payroll full time—vacation	15,000	13,900				
Payroll full time—sick	3,500	3,450				
Payroll seasonal—regular	48,500	46,400				
Kitchen payroll—regular	215,000	211,500				
Kitchen payroll—overtime	27,500	26,000				
Kitchen payroll—holiday	3,200	3,000				
Kitchen payroll—vacation	8,750	8,700				
Snack bar—regular	45,000	44,500				
Snack bar—overtime	3,500	3,250				
Snack bar—vacation	1,200	950				
Leased employees	1,600	1,350	965,000	948,850		Salaries and wages
Less: service charges	(223,890)	(221,425)	(223,890)	(221,425)		Less: service charges
Total payroll	741,110	727,425	741,110	727,425		
Federal unemployment expense	7,800	7,650				
OASDI expense	105,500	103,700				
State unemployment tax expense	7,800	7,650				
Health insurance	6,500	6,300				
Workers' comp insurance	64,350	63,000				
Payroll related expenses—other			191,950	188,300		Payroll taxes and employee benefits
Employee meals	27,350	26,700	27,350	26,700		Employee's meals
Total payroll taxes and benefits	219,300	215,000				
Total payroll and related	960,410	942,425	960,410	942,425		
China	10,500	9,350	20,300	15,525	1	China, glassware and silver
Cleaning supplies	6,500	6,750			11	
Computer expenses—other	7,500	7,500	8,250	8,150	2	Computer expense
Computer lease	1,500	1,500			2	
Contract services	1,500	1,500	1,500	1,500	3	Contract services

USFRC COUNTRY CLUB
TRIAL BALANCE
YEARS ENDED DECEMBER 31, 20X2 AND 20X1

Account	20X2	20X1	Ref.
Copying	150	125	13
Data processing supplies	750	650	2
Dry cleaning supplies			9
Dues and subscriptions	650	600	4
Employee housing			12
Equipment lease	3,200	3,000	5
Equipment repair and maintenance	750	1,050	6
General supplies—other			11
Glassware	3,500	2,850	1
Gratis	850	925	7
Guest supplies	2,200	2,500	11
Kitchen fuel	2,400	2,350	8
Laundry supplies	18,750	17,950	9
Licenses and permits	1,600	1,600	10
Linens	14,000	6,640	9
Loss and damage	350	150	12
Menus	6,200	6,000	13
Miscellaneous	450	350	12
Paper supplies	5,500	5,250	11
Silver	4,800	2,050	1
Spoiled or damaged goods	900	100	12
Training and education	3,200	3,000	14
Uniforms and dry cleaning expense	3,500	3,450	15
Utensils	1,500	1,275	1
Total other	**101,200**	**86,965**	
Total expenses	**1,724,865**	**1,702,435**	
Profit (loss)	**(292,015)**	**(285,735)**	

Grouped summary lines:

Line	20X2	20X1
Dues and subscriptions	650	600
Equipment rental	3,200	3,000
Equipment repairs and maintenance	750	1,050
Gratis food	850	925
Operating supplies	14,200	14,500
Kitchen fuel	2,400	2,350
Laundry and linen	32,750	24,590
Licenses and permits	1,600	1,600
Other operating expenses	1,700	600
Printing and stationery	6,350	6,125
Professional development	3,200	3,000
	3,500	3,450

BEVERAGE

Account	20X2	20X1
Beverage—a la carte	316,700	312,100
Beverage—club event	21,600	21,300
Beverage—banquet	73,000	75,000

USFRC COUNTRY CLUB
TRIAL BALANCE
YEARS ENDED DECEMBER 31, 20X2 AND 20X1

Account	20X2	20X1	20X2	20X1		Statement line	20X2	20X1
Beverage—snack bars	27,400	26,300				Beverage sales		
Beverage—tournaments								
Total beverage revenue	438,700	434,700	438,700	434,700		Total beverage revenue		
Purchases	144,800	144,625	144,800	144,625		Cost of beverage sold		
Total beverage cost of sale	144,800	144,625	144,800	144,625		Total beverage cost of sale		
Gross profit	293,900	290,075	293,900	290,075				
Payroll—management and supervisors	70,100	68,800						
Payroll full time—regular	28,500	27,300						
Payroll full time—vacation	1,750	1,650						
Payroll full time—sick	375	250						
Payroll seasonal—regular	12,000	11,300						
Leased employees	400	350	113,125	109,650		Salaries and wages		
Less: service charges	(74,580)	(73,900)	(74,580)	(73,900)		Less: Service charges		
Total payroll	38,545	35,750	38,545	35,750		Total payroll		
Federal unemployment expense	280	300						
OASDI expense	8,630	8,400						
State unemployment tax expense	280	300						
Workers' comp insurance	5,890	5,800	15,080	14,800		Total payroll taxes and benefits		
Employee meals	1,470	1,340	1,470	1,340		Employee meals		
Total payroll taxes and benefits	16,550	16,140	16,550	16,140				
Total payroll and related	55,095	51,890	55,095	51,890		Total payroll and related		
Contract services	1,200	1,050	1,200	1,050	2	Contract services		
Dues and subscriptions	105	95	105	95	3	Dues and subscriptions		
Equipment lease	1,140	1,140	1,140	1,140	4	Equipment rental		
Equipment repairs	300	450	300	450	5	Equipment repairs and maintenance		
General supplies—other	850	1,050						
Glassware	3,450	2,800	3,450	2,800	1	China, glassware, and silverware		
Gratis	520	750	520	750	6	Gratis food		
Guest supplies	475	425			9			
Laundry supplies	1,200	1,020	1,200	1,020	7	Laundry and linen		

USFRC COUNTRY CLUB
TRIAL BALANCE
YEARS ENDED DECEMBER 31, 20X2 AND 20X1

Account					Ref	Statement line
Licenses and permits	650	650	650		8	Licenses and permits
Miscellaneous	250	375	375		10	Other operating expenses
Paper supplies	2,100	1,950	3,425	3,425	9	Operating supplies
Training and education	300	250	300	250	11	Professional development
Uniforms and dry cleaning expense	450	375	450	375	12	Uniforms
Total other	12,990	12,380	12,990	12,380		
Total expenses	68,085	64,270	68,085	64,270		
Profit (loss)	225,815	225,805	225,815	225,805		
ENTERTAINMENT						
Activity/program fee revenues	5,250	4,800				
Entertainment revenues	10,000	8,500				
Total revenue	15,250	13,300	15,250	13,300		Total revenue
Payroll—management and supervisors	37,500	35,000				
Payroll full time—vacation	1,440	1,350				
Total payroll	38,940	36,350	38,940	36,350		Total salaries and wages
Federal unemployment expense	60	60				
OASDI expense	2,980	2,780				
State unemployment tax expense	60	60				
Workers' comp insurance	2,025	1,890				
Payroll related expenses—other			5,125	4,790		Payroll taxes and benefits
Employee meals	650	650	650	650		Employee meals
Total payroll taxes and benefits	5,775	5,440				
Total payroll and related	44,715	41,790				
Agency fees—entertainment	3,500	3,500	3,500		1	Other operating expenses
Bands—live	27,500	26,500	55,600	55,500	4	Contract entertainment
Cable TV	1,220	1,190	1,190		2	Other operating expenses
Committee supplies	1,500	1,450	1,450		3	Committee expenses
Decorating	7,500	6,900	10,350	11,100	5	Decorations
Decorations—other	3,600	3,450			5	
Entertainment—club event	13,000	13,050			4	

USFRC COUNTRY CLUB
TRIAL BALANCE
YEARS ENDED DECEMBER 31, 20X2 AND 20X1

Account	20X2	20X1	20X2	20X1	Ref	Caption
Entertainment—other	1,550					
Entertainment—special event	15,000	14,500				
Gratis	1,700	1,650	1,700	1,650	4	Gratis
Lettering and engraving	650	635	1,850	1,835	4	Prizes
Training and education	250	250	250	250	6	Professional development
Trophies	1,200	1,200			7	Prizes
Total other expense	76,620	75,825	76,620	75,825	8	Total other expense
Total expenses	121,335	117,615	121,335	117,615		
Net expense	(106,085)	(104,315)	(106,085)	(104,315)		
OVERNIGHT ROOMS						
Rooms—transient—guest	12,500	11,750				
Rooms—transient—member	13,300	13,200	25,800	24,950		Transient
Rooms—permanent	24,000	24,000	24,000	24,000		Permanent
Total revenue	49,800	48,950	49,800	48,950		
Payroll full time—regular	24,000	22,000				
Leased employees	24,000	22,000	24,000	22,000		Total salaries and wages
Total payroll	24,000	22,000				
Federal unemployment expense	110	110				
OASDI expense	1,850	1,700				
State unemployment tax expense	110	110				
Payroll related expenses—other	1,300	1,250	2,070	1,920		
Employee meals	1,300	1,250	1,300	1,250		Total taxes and benefits / Employee meals
Total payroll taxes and benefits	3,370	3,170	3,370	3,170		
Total payroll and related	27,370	25,170	27,370	25,170		
Cleaning supplies	480	450	1,280	1,450	1	Other operating expenses
Dues and subscriptions	125	120	125	120	1	Dues and subscriptions
General supplies—other	800	350				
Gratis	1,750	1,850	1,750	1,850	2	Gratis
Guest supplies	2,200	1,450	2,575	1,870	2	Operating supplies
Linens	7,500	8,200	12,000	12,400	3	Laundry and linen

USFRC COUNTRY CLUB
TRIAL BALANCE
YEARS ENDED DECEMBER 31, 20X2 AND 20X1

Account	20X2	20X1	Ref		Account	20X1
Miscellaneous						
Paper supplies		420				
Telephone	375	650	1		Telephone	
Towels and amenities	2,140	2,060	2			
Training and education	4,500	4,200	3		Professional development	
Uniforms and dry cleaning expense	800	750			Uniforms	
Total other expense	2,400	2,400				
Total expenses	23,070	22,900				
	50,440	48,070				
Net income (expense)	(640)	880				

GOLF OPERATIONS

Account	20X2	20X1		Account	20X1
Guest fees—golf	14,300	13,350		Guest fees—golf	13,350
Greens fees	340,000	339,400		Greens fees	339,400
Cart fee revenue	120,000	118,900		Cart fee revenue	118,900
Trail fees	6,500	6,350		Trail fees	6,350
Club storage revenue—golf	60,000	59,500		Club storage revenue—golf	59,500
Clinics and lessons—golf	36,000	34,250		Clinics and lessons—golf	34,250
Club and cart repairs	13,200	13,350		Club and cart repairs	13,350
Total revenue	590,000	585,100		Total revenue	585,100
Payroll—management and supervisors	125,000	119,000			
Payroll full time—regular	65,000	63,200			
Total payroll	190,000	182,200		Total salaries and wages	182,200
Federal unemployment expense	390	370			
OASDI expense	12,240	10,200			
State unemployment tax expense	390	370			
Payroll related expenses—other	4,200	4,120			
Employee meals	13,020			Total taxes and benefits	15,060
Total payroll taxes and benefits	17,220	15,060		Employee meals	4,120
Total payroll and related	207,220	197,260			
Cart expense	23,900	23,200		Golf cart repairs and maintenance	23,200
Clubhouse electricity	6,000	5,890		Electricity	5,890

USFRC COUNTRY CLUB
TRIAL BALANCE
YEARS ENDED DECEMBER 31, 20X2 AND 20X1

Committee supplies	750	950	750	950	Other operating expenses
Computer expenses—other	3,200	3,150	3,200	3,150	Computer expense
Contract professionals	7,500	7,000	7,500	7,000	Contract professionals
Dues and subscriptions	750	745	750	745	Dues and subscriptions
Equipment lease	4,800	4,800	4,800	4,800	Equipment lease
General supplies—other	6,800	6,750	6,800	6,750	Operating supplies
Laundry supplies	4,350	4,000			
Towels and amenities	2,200	2,350	6,550	6,350	Laundry and linen [1]
Training and education	2,000	1,850	2,000	1,850	Professional development [1]
Uniforms and dry cleaning expense	3,200	3,200	3,200	3,200	Uniforms
Total other expense	65,450	63,885	65,450	63,885	
Total expenses	272,670	261,145	272,670	261,145	
Net income (expense)	317,330	323,955	317,330	323,955	

GOLF SHOP

Pro shop equipment	105,000	97,500			
Pro shop accessories	48,500	53,100			
Pro shop apparel	74,350	77,000			
Pro shop logo merchandise	52,000	47,000			
Golf merchandise — Sales	279,850	274,600	279,850	274,600	Sales
Golf merchandise	223,820	219,700	223,820	219,700	Cost of sales
Gross profit	56,030	54,900	56,030	54,900	Gross profit
Payroll full time—regular	36,000	33,000	36,000	33,000	
Total payroll	36,000	33,000			
Federal unemployment expense	100	100			
OASDI expense	2,750	2,500			
State unemployment tax expense	100	100			
Payroll related expenses—other			2,950	2,700	
Employee meals	1,300	1,380	1,300	1,380	Total taxes and benefits
Total payroll taxes and benefits	4,250	4,080	4,250	4,080	Employee meals
Total payroll and related	40,250	37,080	40,250	37,080	

USFRC COUNTRY CLUB
TRIAL BALANCE
YEARS ENDED DECEMBER 31, 20X2 AND 20X1

Account	20X2	20X1	20X2	20X1	Reclassified account	Ref
Data processing supplies	550	650	550	650	Computer expense	
Dues and subscriptions	780	780	780	780	Dues and subscriptions	
Equipment lease	1,200	1,200	1,200	1,200	Equipment rental	
General supplies—other	1,780	1,650	1,780	1,650	Operating supplies	
Gratis	1,200	1,150	1,200	1,150	Gratis food	
Telephone	1,250	1,175	1,250	1,175	Telephone	
Training and education	450	400	450	400	Professional development	
Uniforms and dry cleaning expense	1,200	1,200	1,200	1,200	Uniforms	
Total other expense	8,410	8,205	8,410	8,205		
Total expenses	48,660	45,285	48,660	45,285		
Net income (expense)	7,370	9,615	7,370	9,615		

GOLF COURSE MAINTENANCE

Account	20X2	20X1	20X2	20X1	Reclassified account	Ref
Payroll—management and supervisors	165,000	154,500				
Payroll full time—regular	295,000	285,500				
Payroll full time—overtime	42,500	45,000				
Payroll full time—holiday	17,500	16,300				
Payroll full time—vacation	9,800	8,700				
Payroll full time—sick	3,500	3,250				
Payroll seasonal—regular	42,000	38,500				
Total payroll	575,300	551,750	575,300	551,750	Total salaries and wages	
Federal unemployment expense	2,200	2,300				
OASDI expense	67,450	66,300				
State unemployment tax expense	2,200	2,300				
Payroll related expenses—other	71,850	70,900				
Employee meals	6,400	6,250			Employee meals	
Total payroll taxes and benefits	78,250	77,150	78,250	77,150	Total taxes and benefits	
Total payroll and related	653,550	628,900	653,550	628,900		
Chemicals	4,300	4,250				
Computer expenses—other	1,350	1,050			Computer expense	1
Course applicants	50,200	49,250			Applicants	1

USFRC COUNTRY CLUB
TRIAL BALANCE
YEARS ENDED DECEMBER 31, 20X2 AND 20X1

Account	20X2	20X2	20X1	20X1	Reclassified account
Dues and subscriptions	2,200	2,200	2,100	2,100	Dues and subscriptions
Electricity, other	22,100	22,100	20,900	20,900	Energy
Equipment rental	27,500	27,500	25,000	25,000	Equipment rental
Fertilizers	51,000	51,000	49,500	49,500	Fertilizer
Gasoline and lubricants	20,500	20,500	19,900	19,900	Gasoline and lubricants
Irrigation and drainage	4,500	4,500	4,350	4,350	Drainage [2]
Landscaping	3,500		3,300		
Licenses and permits	650	650	650	650	Licenses and permits
Mechanical repairs	45,300	45,300	44,200	44,200	Mowers, tractors, etc
Miscellaneous	7,350	7,350	6,950	6,950	Other operating expenses
Roads and paths	500	500	450	450	Roads and paths
Sand and gravel	11,500	15,000	12,300	15,600	Sand and topsoil dressing [2]
Seeds, flowers, shrubs	4,200	4,200	3,200	3,200	Seeds, flowers, shrubs
Telephone	1,250	1,250	1,175	1,175	Telephone
Training and education	3,500	3,500	3,420	3,420	Professional development
Uniforms and dry cleaning expense	9,200	9,200	9,050	9,050	Uniforms
Vehicle expenses	1,100		975		
Vehicle lease	6,540	7,640	6,540	7,515	Vehicle expense
Refuse removal	8,350	8,350	8,150	8,150	Refuse removal
Total other expense	286,590	286,590	276,660	276,660	
Total expenses	940,140	940,140	905,560	905,560	

RACQUET SPORTS

Account	20X2	20X2	20X1	20X1	Reclassified account
Guest fees—racquets	3,500	4,950	3,450	5,150	Court fees
Activity/program fee revenues	1,450	1,700			Rentals
Rentals	380	420	380	420	
Total revenue	5,330	5,570	5,330	5,570	Total revenue
Payroll—management and supervisors	35,040	34,020	35,040	34,020	Total wages
Total payroll	35,040	34,020	35,040	34,020	
Federal unemployment expense	100	100			
OASDI expense	2,680	2,600			
State unemployment tax expense	100	100			
Workers' comp insurance	1,800	1,800			

USFRC COUNTRY CLUB
TRIAL BALANCE
YEARS ENDED DECEMBER 31, 20X2 AND 20X1

Account	20X2	20X1	20X2	20X1	Reclassification
Payroll related expenses—other	1,400		4,680	4,600	Total taxes and benefits
Employee meals	1,350		1,400	1,350	Employees' meal
Total payroll taxes and benefits	6,080	5,950	6,080	5,950	
Total payroll and related	41,120	39,970	41,120	39,970	Total
Committee supplies	6,300	4,300	6,300	4,300	Other operating expenses
Court maintenance	4,000	4,100	4,000	4,100	Court maintenance
Dues and subscriptions	120	120	120	120	Dues and subscriptions
Gratis	450	425	450	425	Gratis
Linens	1,600	1,450	1,600	1,450	Laundry
Training and education	250	200	250	200	Professional development
Total other expense	12,720	10,595	12,720	10,595	
Total expenses	53,840	50,565	53,840	50,565	
Net income (expense)	(48,510)	(44,995)	(48,510)	(44,995)	

AQUATIC SPORTS

Account	20X2	20X1	20X2	20X1	Reclassification
Guest fees—aquatic	3,500	3,250	4,200	3,900	Revenue
Activity/program fee revenues	700	650	280	320	Other
Towel fees	280	320	4,480	4,220	
Total revenue	4,480	4,220			
Payroll full time—regular	15,250	15,000	15,250	15,000	
Federal unemployment expense	1,700	1,700			
OASDI expense	1,200	1,200			
State unemployment tax expense	1,700	1,700			
Workers' comp insurance	800	800			
Payroll related expenses—other			5,400	5,400	Total taxes and benefits
Employee meals	620	580	620	580	Employees' meals
Total payroll taxes and benefits	6,020	5,980	6,020	5,980	
Total payroll and related	21,270	20,980	21,270	20,980	
Committee supplies	300	350	300	350	Other operating expenses
Equipment repairs	2,000	1,500	2,000	1,500	Equipment repairs and maintenance

USFRC COUNTRY CLUB
TRIAL BALANCE
YEARS ENDED DECEMBER 31, 20X2 AND 20X1

Account	20X2	20X1		Account	20X2	20X1
General supplies—other	7,250	7,100		Operating supplies	7,250	7,100
Gratis	450	425		Gratis	450	425
Laundry supplies	3,000	2,000		Laundry supplies	4,880	3,060
Licenses and permits	180	180		Licenses and permits [1]	180	180
Towels and amenities	1,880	1,060				
Training and education	150	120		Professional development	150	120
Trophies	1,200	1,200		Prizes	1,200	1,200
Uniforms and dry cleaning expense	320	300		Uniforms	320	300
Total other expense	16,730	14,235		Total other expense	16,730	14,235
Total expenses	38,000	35,215		Total expenses	38,000	35,215
Net income (expense)	(33,520)	(30,995)		Net (expense) [1]	(33,520)	(30,995)

LOCKER ROOMS

Account	20X2	20X1		Account	20X2	20X1
Locker rental—members	97,800	92,900				
Total revenue	97,800	92,900				
Payroll full time—regular	69,700	67,700				
Federal unemployment expense	170	170				
OASDI expense	5,185	5,180				
State unemployment tax expense	170	170				
Workers' comp insurance	3,620	3,520				
Payroll related expenses—other				Total taxes and benefits [1]	9,145	9,040
Employee meals	2,200	2,150		Employees' meals	2,200	2,150
Total payroll taxes and benefits	11,345	11,190				
Total payroll and related	81,045	78,890				
Cleaning supplies	1,100	1,050		Operating supplies [1]	4,000	4,200
Gratis	8,000	7,950		Gratis food	7,950	8,000
Guest supplies	7,100	7,050		Member supplies	7,050	7,100
Laundry supplies	9,980	9,950		Laundry and linen	9,950	9,980
Miscellaneous	3,100	2,950				
Uniforms and dry cleaning expense	400	380		Uniforms	380	400

USFRC COUNTRY CLUB
TRIAL BALANCE
YEARS ENDED DECEMBER 31, 20X2 AND 20X1

					Ref	Reclassified
Total other expense	29,680	29,330	29,680	29,330		Total other expense
Total expenses	110,725	108,220	110,725	108,220		Total expenses
Net income (expense)	(12,925)	(15,320)	(12,925)	(15,320)		Net (expense)
RENTAL AND OTHER						
Masseuse concession	2,400	2,400	2,400	2,400		Space rentals and concessions
Interest income	22,050	19,900	22,050	19,900		Interest income
Late charges	7,550	7,490	7,550	7,490		Member late fees
Discounts earned	150	130	150	130		Cash discounts earned
Total rental and other revenue	32,150	29,920	32,150	29,920		
ADMINISTRATIVE AND GENERAL						
Payroll—management and supervisors	260,000	252,400				
Payroll full time—regular	145,000	139,900				
Total payroll	405,000	392,300	405,000	392,300		Total salary and wages
Federal unemployment expense	670	670				
OASDI expense	33,300	32,300				
State unemployment tax expense	670	670				
Workers' comp insurance	22,620	22,000				
Payroll related expenses—other			57,260	55,640		
Employee meals	4,400	4,250	4,400	4,250		Employees' meals
Total payroll taxes and benefits	61,660	59,890	61,660	59,890		Payroll taxes and benefits
Total payroll and related	466,660	452,190	466,660	452,190		
Contract maintenance—hardware	4,200	4,200			2	Computer expense
Contract maintenance—software	3,500	3,250	7,700	7,450	2	Credit card fees
Credit card fees	770	690	770	690	3	Dues and subscriptions
Dues and subscriptions	6,500	6,350	6,500	6,350	4	Equipment rental
Equipment lease	3,180	3,180	3,180	3,180	5	Other
General supplies—other	7,450	7,380	7,450	7,380		Licenses and permits
Licenses and permits	4,100	3,950	4,100	3,950	6	Loss and damage
Loss and damage	670	550	670	550	7	Club publications
Newsletters	17,500	16,950	17,500	16,950	1	

USFRC COUNTRY CLUB
TRIAL BALANCE
YEARS ENDED DECEMBER 31, 20X2 AND 20X1

	20X2	20X1	20X2	20X1	Ref	Account
Postage	13,020	12,080	13,020	12,080	8	Postage
Printing	12,050	12,320	12,050	12,320	9	Printing and stationery
Professional fees — accounting	20,000	19,050			10	
Professional fees — legal	850	450	20,850	19,500	10	Professional fees
Provision for doubtful accounts	10,200	8,500	10,200	8,500	12	Provision for doubtful accounts
Telephone	22,200	22,750	22,200	22,750	13	Telephone
Training and education	3,500	3,350	3,500	3,350	11	Professional development
Trade association conferences	4,000	4,000	4,000	4,000	14	Trade association conferences
Vehicle expenses	3,750	3,840			15	
Vehicle lease	6,300	6,300	10,050	10,140	15	Vehicle expenses
Website development	7,500	2,400	7,500	2,400	16	
Total other expense	151,240	141,540	151,240	141,540		
Total administrative and general	617,900	593,730	617,900	593,730		

ENERGY

	20X2	20X1	20X2	20X1		Account
Clubhouse electricity	76,250	75,750	76,250	75,750		Electricity
Propane	33,500	33,110	33,500	33,110		Fuel
Water—main	3,370	3,130	3,370	3,130		Water
Total energy	113,120	111,990	113,120	111,990		

FACILITY MAINTENANCE

	20X2	20X1	20X2	20X1		Account
Payroll—management and supervisors	65,000	63,100				
Payroll full time— regular	151,000	146,600				
Total payroll	216,000	209,700	216,000	209,700		
Federal unemployment expense	450	450				
OASDI expense	16,500	16,040				
State unemployment tax expense	450	450				
Workers' comp insurance	11,200	10,900				
Payroll related expenses—other	4,110	4,090	28,600	27,840		Payroll taxes and benefits
Employee meals						Employees' meals
Total payroll taxes and benefits	32,710	31,930	32,710	31,930		
Total payroll and related	248,710	241,630	248,710	241,630		

USFRC COUNTRY CLUB
TRIAL BALANCE
YEARS ENDED DECEMBER 31, 20X2 AND 20X1

Account	20X2	20X1	20X2	20X1	Ref	Reclassified account
Building supplies	11,000	10,900	11,000	10,900	1	Building
Dues and subscriptions	375	355	375	355		Dues and subscriptions
Elevators	1,200	1,200	1,200	1,200		Elevators
Electrical	11,250	10,350	11,250	10,350		Electrical and mechanical equipment
Floor coverings	5,100	5,050	5,100	5,050		Floor coverings
General supplies—other	7,320	7,920			1	
HVAC	12,050	11,950	12,050	11,950		HVAC
Landscaping	3,250	7,040	14,500	18,230	2	Grounds and landscaping
Painting	6,500	6,350	6,500	6,350		Painting and decorating
Pest Control	7,350	6,970	14,670	14,890	1	Other operating expenses
Plumbing	7,800	8,300	7,800	8,300		Plumbing
Seeds, flowers, shrubs	11,250	11,190			2	Grounds and landscaping
Training and education	450	450	450	450		Professional development
Uniforms and dry cleaning expense	3,450	3,390	3,450	3,390		Uniforms
Vehicle expenses	3,350	2,790				
Vehicle lease	5,100	5,100	8,450	7,890		Vehicle expense
Refuse removal	13,950	13,870	13,950	13,870		Refuse removal
Total other expense	110,745	113,175	110,745	113,175		Total other expense
Total facility maintenance	359,455	354,805	359,455	354,805		
Current federal income tax	9,800	3,280	9,800	3,280		Provision for income taxes
Depreciation	555,850	525,750	555,850	525,750		Depreciation expense
Interest	22,500	7,700	22,500	7,700		Interest expense
Other insurance	185,000	145,000	185,000	145,000		Club package insurance
Real estate tax	155,000	147,500	155,000	147,500		Real estate taxes
	928,150	829,230	928,150	829,230		
Balance	—	—	—	—		

Country Club
Statement of Financial Position
Years ended December 31, 20X2 and 20X1

Assets

	20X2	20X1
CURRENT ASSETS		
Cash and cash equivalents	$ 1,053,850	$ 939,000
Short–term investments	20,000	20,000
Receivables:		
Accounts receivable—members	187,600	162,000
Other receivables	9,500	9,200
Total receivables	197,100	171,200
Less allowance for doubtful accounts	(3,000)	(4,000)
Net receivables	194,100	167,200
Inventories	109,500	106,400
Prepaid expenses	76,550	74,450
Total current assets	1,454,000	1,307,050
PROPERTY AND EQUIPMENT		
Land	1,000,000	1,000,000
Construction in progress	–	25,000
Buildings and building improvements	3,405,000	3,275,000
Golf course and golf course improvements	4,550,000	4,400,000
Furniture, fixtures, and equipment	2,160,000	2,069,500
China, glass, silver, linen, and uniforms	31,000	31,000
Total property and equipment	11,146,000	10,800,500
Less accumulated depreciation and amortization	(3,146,000)	(2,590,150)
Net property and equipment	8,000,000	8,210,350
OTHER ASSETS		
Security deposits	5,500	5,500
Other	38,200	43,000
Total other assets	43,700	48,500
TOTAL ASSETS	$ 9,497,700	$ 9,565,900

Country Club
Statement of Financial Position
Years ended December 31, 20X2 and 20X1

Liabilities and Net Assets

	20X2	20X1
CURRENT LIABILITIES		
Notes payable	$ 95,000	$ 100,000
Accounts payable	176,865	190,065
Taxes payable and accrued	182,480	180,885
Accrued expenses	45,000	44,300
Current portion of long-term debt	75,000	75,000
Dues billed in advance	602,000	670,000
Total current liabilities	1,176,345	1,260,250
LONG-TERM DEBT		
Notes payable, net of current maturity	-	95,000
Obligations under capital lease, net of current maturity	50,000	75,000
Mortgage payable, net of current maturity	450,000	500,000
Total liabilities	1,676,345	1,930,250
UNRESTRICTED NET ASSETS (MEMBERS' EQUITY)		
Capital stock	3,000,000	3,000,000
Designated	505,000	400,000
Undesignated	4,316,355	4,235,650
Total unrestricted net assets	7,821,355	7,635,650
TOTAL LIABILITIES AND NET UNRESTRICTED ASSETS	$ 9,497,700	$ 9,565,900

Country Club
Statement of Activities
Years ended December 31, 20X2 and 20X1

	20X2	20X1
REVENUE		
Membership dues	$ 2,805,000	$ 2,550,000
Initiation fees	140,000	130,000
Food	1,432,850	1,416,700
Beverage	438,700	434,700
Entertainment	15,250	13,300
Golf operations	590,000	585,100
Golf shop	279,850	274,600
Racquet sports	5,330	5,570
Aquatic sports	4,480	4,220
Overnight rooms	49,800	48,950
Locker rooms	· 97,800	92,900
Rentals and other revenue	32,150	29,920
Total revenue	5,891,210	5,585,960
OPERATING EXPENSES		
Food	1,724,865	1,702,435
Beverage	212,885	208,895
Entertainment	121,335	117,615
Golf operations	272,670	261,145
Golf shop	272,480	264,985
Golf course maintenance	940,140	905,560
Racquet sports	53,840	50,565
Aquatic sports	38,000	35,215
Overnight rooms	50,440	48,070
Locker rooms	110,725	108,220
Administrative and general	617,900	593,730
Energy costs	113,120	111,990
Facility maintenance	359,455	354,805
Total operating expenses	4,887,855	4,763,230
INCOME BEFORE FIXED CHARGES	1,003,355	822,730
FIXED CHARGES		
Property taxes	155,000	147,500
Insurance	185,000	145,000
Interest	22,500	7,700
Depreciation and amortization	555,850	525,750
Total fixed charges	918,350	825,950
INCOME (LOSS) BEFORE TAXES	85,005	(3,220)
PROVISION FOR INCOME TAXES	9,800	3,280
Results of operations	75,205	(6,500)
OTHER ACTIVITIES		
Capital assessment	105,000	–
Interest earned on board designated funds	5,500	10,000
Total other activities	110,500	10,000
INCREASE IN UNRESTRICTED NET ASSETS	185,705	3,500
UNRESTRICTED NET ASSETS, BEGINNING OF PERIOD	7,635,650	7,632,150
UNRESTRICTED NET ASSETS, END OF PERIOD	$ 7,821,355	$ 7,635,650

Country Club
Statement of Cash Flows
Years ended December 31, 20X2 and 20X1
(INDIRECT APPROACH)

	20X2	20X1
CASH FLOWS FROM OPERATING ACTIVITIES		
Increase in unrestricted net assets	$ 185,705	$ 3,500
Adjustments to reconcile increase (decrease) in net assets to net cash provided (used) by operating activities		
Depreciation and amortization	555,850	525,750
(Increase) decrease in assets		
Accounts receivable		
Accounts receivable—members	(26,600)	3,200
Other receivables	(300)	150
Inventories	(3,100)	(1,050)
Prepaid expenses	(2,100)	450
Other current assets	4,800	–
Increase (decrease) in liabilities		
Accounts payable	(13,200)	(2,500)
Taxes payable and accrued	1,595	(2,300)
Accrued expenses	700	12,000
Dues billed in advance	(68,000)	17,000
Net cash provided by operating activities	635,350	556,200
CASH FLOWS FROM INVESTING ACTIVITIES		
Expenditures for property and equipment	(345,500)	(75,250)
Proceeds from sale of property and equipment	-	7,900
Net cash provided (used) by investing activities	(345,500)	(67,350)
Cash flows from financing activities		
Repayment of debt	(175,000)	(65,000)
Capital stock sold	50,000	30,000
Capital stock redeemed	(50,000)	(30,000)
Net cash (used) by financing activities	(175,000)	(65,000)
NET INCREASE (DECREASE) IN CASH AND CASH EQUIVALENTS	114,850	423,850
CASH AND CASH EQUIVALENTS, BEGINNING OF PERIOD	939,000	515,150
CASH AND CASH EQUIVALENTS, END OF PERIOD	$ 1,053,850	$ 939,000
SUPPLEMENTAL DISCLOSURE OF CASH FLOW INFORMATION:		
Interest paid during the year	$ 22,500	$ 7,700
Income taxes paid during the year	$ 9,800	$ 3,280

Country Club
Statement of Activities
Years ended December 31, 20X2 and 20X1
(IN DEPARTMENTAL FORM)

		Period Ending	
	Schedule	20X2	20X1
MEMBERSHIP REVENUE			
Membership dues		$ 2,805,000	$ 2,550,000
Initiation fees		140,000	130,000
Total membership revenue		2,945,000	2,680,000
COST OF SPORTS ACTIVITIES			
Golf operations income	E	317,330	323,955
Less golf course maintenance	G	(940,140)	(905,560)
Golf shop	F	7,370	9,615
Net golf profit (expense)		(615,440)	(571,990)
Racquet sports	H	(48,510)	(44,995)
Aquatic sports	J	(33,520)	(30,995)
Net cost of sports activities		(697,470)	(647,980)
Revenue available for clubhouse operations and fixed charges		2,247,530	2,032,020
CLUBHOUSE OPERATING INCOME (LOSS)			
Food	A	(292,015)	(285,735)
Beverage	B	225,815	225,805
Entertainment	C	(106,085)	(104,315)
Overnight rooms	D	(640)	880
Locker rooms	L	(12,925)	(15,320)
Rentals and other revenue	O	32,150	29,920
Total clubhouse operating income (loss)		(153,700)	(148,765)
UNDISTRIBUTED OPERATING EXPENSES			
Administrative and general	P	617,900	593,730
Energy costs	R	113,120	111,990
Facility maintenance	R	359,455	354,805
Total undistributed operating expenses		1,090,475	1,060,525
Clubhouse operations and undistributed operating expenses		(1,244,175)	(1,209,290)
INCOME BEFORE FIXED CHARGES		1,003,355	822,730
FIXED CHARGES			
Property taxes		155,000	147,500
Insurance		185,000	145,000
Interest		22,500	7,700
Depreciation and amortization		555,850	525,750
Total fixed charges		918,350	825,950
INCOME (LOSS) BEFORE INCOME TAXES		85,005	(3,220)
PROVISION FOR INCOME TAXES		9,800	3,280
Results of operations		75,205	(6,500)
OTHER ACTIVITIES			
Capital assessment		105,000	–
Interest earned on board designated funds		5,500	10,000
Total other activities		110,500	10,000
INCREASE IN UNRESTRICTED NET ASSETS		185,705	3,500
UNRESTRICTED NET ASSETS, BEGINNING OF PERIOD		7,635,650	7,632,150
UNRESTRICTED NET ASSETS, END OF PERIOD		$ 7,821,355	$ 7,635,650

Food—Schedule A
Years ended December 31, 20X2 and 20X1

	Period Ending			
	20X2	20X1		
FOOD SALES	$ 1,417,000	$ 1,402,500	100.00%	100.00%
COST OF FOOD SOLD				
Cost of food consumed	731,825	747,330	51.65%	53.29%
Less credit for employees' meals	(55,400)	(54,110)	-3.91%	-3.86%
Less credit for gratis food	(13,170)	(20,175)	-0.93%	-1.44%
Cost of food sold	663,255	673,045	46.81%	47.99%
Gross profit on food sales	753,745	729,455	53.19%	52.01%
OTHER REVENUE				
Unused minimum	7,500	7,250	0.53%	1.08%
Dining room rental	8,350	6,950	0.59%	1.03%
Total other revenue	15,850	14,200	1.12%	2.11%
Total gross profit and other revenue	769,595	743,655	54.31%	53.02%
DEPARTMENTAL EXPENSES				
Payroll and related expenses				
Salaries and wages	965,000	948,850	68.10%	67.65%
Less service charges	(223,890)	(221,425)	-15.80%	-15.79%
Payroll taxes and employee benefits	191,950	188,300	13.55%	13.43%
Employees' meals	27,350	26,700	1.93%	1.90%
Total payroll and related expenses	960,410	942,425	67.78%	67.20%
OTHER EXPENSES				
China, glassware, and silver	20,300	15,525	1.43%	1.11%
Computer expense	8,250	8,150	0.58%	0.58%
Contract services	1,500	1,500	0.11%	0.11%
Dues and subscriptions	650	600	0.05%	0.04%
Equipment rental	3,200	3,000	0.23%	0.21%
Equipment repair and maintenance	750	1,050	0.05%	0.07%
Gratis food	850	925	0.06%	0.07%
Kitchen fuel	2,400	2,350	0.17%	0.17%
Laundry and linen	32,750	24,590	2.31%	1.75%
Licenses and permits	1,600	1,600	0.11%	0.11%
Operating supplies	14,200	14,500	1.00%	1.03%
Printing and stationery	6,350	6,125	0.45%	0.44%
Professional development	3,200	3,000	0.23%	0.21%
Uniforms	3,500	3,450	0.25%	0.25%
Other operating expenses	1,700	600	0.12%	0.04%
Total other expenses	101,200	86,965	7.14%	6.20%
TOTAL DEPARTMENTAL EXPENSES	1,061,610	1,029,390	74.92%	73.40%
DEPARTMENTAL (LOSS)	$ (292,015)	$ (285,735)	-20.61%	-20.37%

Beverage—Schedule B
Years ended December 31, 20X2 and 20X1

	Period Ending			
	20X2	**20X1**		
BEVERAGE SALES	$ 438,700	$ 434,700	100.00%	100.00%
COST OF BEVERAGE SOLD	144,800	144,625	33.01%	33.27%
Gross profit on beverage sales	293,900	290,075	66.99%	66.73%
DEPARTMENTAL EXPENSES				
Payroll and related expenses				
Salaries and wages	113,125	109,650	25.79%	25.22%
Less service charges	(74,580)	(73,900)	−17.00%	−17.00%
Payroll taxes and employee benefits	15,080	14,800	3.44%	3.40%
Employees' meals	1,470	1,340	0.34%	0.31%
Total payroll and related expenses	55,095	51,890	12.56%	11.94%
OTHER EXPENSES				
China, glassware, and silver	3,450	2,800	0.79%	0.64%
Contract services	1,200	1,050	0.27%	0.24%
Dues and subscriptions	105	95	0.02%	0.02%
Equipment rental	1,140	1,140	0.26%	0.26%
Equipment repair and maintenance	300	450	0.07%	0.10%
Gratis food	520	750	0.12%	0.17%
Laundry and linen	1,200	1,020	0.27%	0.23%
Licenses and permits	650	650	0.15%	0.15%
Operating supplies	250	375	0.06%	0.09%
Professional development	300	250	0.07%	0.06%
Uniforms	450	375	0.10%	0.09%
Other operating expenses	3,425	3,425	0.78%	0.79%
Total other expenses	12,990	12,380	2.96%	2.85%
TOTAL DEPARTMENTAL EXPENSES	68,085	64,270	15.52%	14.78%
DEPARTMENTAL INCOME	$ 225,815	$ 225,805	51.47%	51.95%

Combined Food and Beverage—Schedule A&B
Years ended December 31, 20X2 and 20X1

	Period Ending			
	20X2	**20X1**		
FOOD SALES	1,417,000	1,402,500	100.00%	100.00%
COST OF FOOD SOLD				
Cost of food consumed	$ 731,825	$ 747,330	51.65%	53.29%
Less credit for employees' meals	(55,400)	(54,110)	−3.91%	−3.86%
Less credit for gratis food	(13,170)	(20,175)	−0.93%	−1.44%
Cost of food sold	663,255	673,045	46.81%	47.99%
Gross profit on food sales	753,745	729,455	53.19%	52.01%
BEVERAGE SALES	438,700	434,700	100.00%	100.00%
COST OF BEVERAGE SOLD	144,800	144,625	33.01%	33.27%
Gross profit on beverage sales	293,900	290,075	66.99%	66.73%
COMBINED FOOD AND BEVERAGE SALES	1,855,700	1,837,200	100.00%	100.00%
COMBINED COST OF FOOD CONSUMED	808,055	817,670	43.54%	44.51%
Combined gross profit	1,047,645	1,019,530	56.46%	55.49%
OTHER REVENUE				
Unused minimum	7,500	7,250	0.40%	0.39%
Dining room rental	8,350	6,950	0.45%	0.38%
Total other revenue	15,850	14,200	0.85%	0.77%
Total gross profit and other revenue	1,063,495	1,033,730	57.31%	56.27%
DEPARTMENTAL EXPENSES				
Payroll and related expenses				
Salaries and wages	1,078,125	1,058,500	58.10%	57.61%
Less service charges	(298,470)	(295,325)	−16.08%	−16.07%
Payroll taxes and employee benefits	207,030	203,100	11.16%	11.05%
Employees' meals	28,820	28,040	1.55%	1.53%
Total payroll and related expenses	1,015,505	994,315	54.72%	54.12%
Other expenses				
China, glassware, and silver	23,750	18,325	1.28%	1.00%
Computer expense	8,250	8,150	0.44%	0.44%
Contract services	2,700	2,550	0.15%	0.14%
Dues and subscriptions	755	695	0.04%	0.04%
Equipment rental	4,340	4,140	0.23%	0.23%
Equipment repair and maintenance	1,050	1,500	0.06%	0.08%
Gratis food	1,370	1,675	0.07%	0.09%
Kitchen fuel	2,400	2,350	0.13%	0.13%
Laundry and linen	33,950	25,610	1.83%	1.39%
Licenses and permits	2,250	2,250	0.12%	0.12%
Operating supplies	14,450	14,875	0.78%	0.81%
Printing and stationery	6,350	6,125	0.34%	0.33%
Professional development	3,500	3,250	0.19%	0.18%
Uniforms	3,950	3,825	0.21%	0.21%
Other operating expenses	5,125	4,025	0.28%	0.22%
Total other expenses	114,190	99,345	6.15%	5.41%
TOTAL DEPARTMENTAL EXPENSES	1,129,695	1,093,660	60.88%	59.53%
DEPARTMENTAL (LOSS)	$ (66,200)	$ (59,930)	−3.57%	−3.26%
FOOD TO BEVERAGE SALES RATIO	3.23 to 1	3.23 to 1		

Entertainment—Schedule C
Years ended December 31, 20X2 and 20X1

	Period Ending	
	20X2	**20X1**
REVENUE	$ 15,250	$ 13,300
DEPARTMENTAL EXPENSES		
Payroll and related expenses		
Salaries and wages	38,940	36,350
Payroll taxes and employee benefits	5,125	4,790
Employees' meals	650	650
Total payroll and employee benefits	44,715	41,790
Other expenses		
Committee expenses	1,500	1,450
Contract entertainment	55,500	55,600
Decorations and props	11,100	10,350
Gratis food	1,700	1,650
Prizes	1,850	1,835
Professional development	250	250
Other operating expenses	4,720	4,690
Total other expenses	76,620	75,825
TOTAL DEPARTMENTAL EXPENSES	121,335	117,615
DEPARTMENTAL (LOSS)	$ (106,085)	$ (104,315)

Overnight Rooms—Schedule D

Years ended December 31, 20X2 and 20X1

	Period Ending	
	20X2	**20X1**
REVENUE		
Transient	$ 25,800	$ 24,950
Permanent	24,000	24,000
Total revenue	49,800	48,950
DEPARTMENTAL EXPENSES		
Payroll and related expenses		
Salaries and wages	24,000	22,000
Payroll taxes and employee benefits	2,070	1,920
Employees' meals	1,300	1,250
Total payroll and related expenses	27,370	25,170
Other expenses		
Dues and subscriptions	125	120
Gratis food	1,750	1,850
Laundry and linen	12,000	12,400
Operating supplies	2,575	1,870
Professional development	800	750
Telephone	2,140	2,060
Uniforms	2,400	2,400
Other operating expenses	1,280	1,450
Total other expenses	23,070	22,900
TOTAL DEPARTMENTAL EXPENSES	50,440	48,070
DEPARTMENTAL INCOME (LOSS)	$ (640)	$ 880

Golf Operations—Schedule E

Years ended December 31, 20X2 and 20X1

	Period Ending	
	20X2	**20X1**
REVENUE		
Greens fees	$ 340,000	$ 339,400
Guest fees	14,300	13,350
Trail fees	6,500	6,350
Club storage	60,000	59,500
Cart rentals	120,000	118,900
Service of member-owned carts and clubs	13,200	13,350
Lessons	36,000	34,250
Total revenue	590,000	585,100
DEPARTMENTAL EXPENSES		
Payroll and related expenses		
Salaries and wages	190,000	182,200
Payroll taxes and employee benefits	13,020	10,940
Employees' meals	4,200	4,120
Total payroll and related expenses	207,220	197,260
Other expenses		
Computer expense	3,200	3,150
Contract professionals	7,500	7,000
Dues and subscriptions	750	745
Electricity	6,000	5,890
Equipment rental	4,800	4,800
Golf cart repairs and maintenance	23,900	23,200
Laundry and linen	6,550	6,350
Operating supplies	6,800	6,750
Professional development	2,000	1,850
Uniforms	3,200	3,200
Other operating expenses	750	950
Total other expenses	65,450	63,885
TOTAL DEPARTMENTAL EXPENSES	272,670	261,145
DEPARTMENTAL INCOME	$ 317,330	$ 323,955

Golf Shop—Schedule F

Years ended December 31, 20X2 and 20X1

	Period Ending	
	20X2	**20X1**
REVENUE	$ 279,850	$ 274,600
COST OF MERCHANDISE SOLD	223,820	219,700
Gross profit on golf shop revenue	56,030	54,900
DEPARTMENTAL EXPENSES		
Payroll and related expenses		
Salaries and wages	36,000	33,000
Payroll taxes and employee benefits	2,950	2,700
Employees' meals	1,300	1,380
Total payroll and related expenses	40,250	37,080
Other expenses		
Computer expense	550	650
Dues and subscriptions	780	780
Equipment rental	1,200	1,200
Gratis food	1,200	1,150
Operating supplies	1,780	1,650
Professional development	450	400
Telephone	1,250	1,175
Uniforms	1,200	1,200
Total other expenses	8,410	8,205
TOTAL DEPARTMENTAL EXPENSES	48,660	45,285
DEPARTMENTAL INCOME	$ 7,370	$ 9,615

Golf Course Maintenance—Schedule G
Years ended December 31, 20X2 and 20X1

	Period Ending	
	20X2	**20X1**
DEPARTMENTAL EXPENSES		
Payroll and related expenses		
Salaries and wages	$ 575,300	$ 551,750
Payroll taxes and employee benefits	71,850	70,900
Employees' meals	6,400	6,250
Total payroll and related expenses	653,550	628,900
Other expenses		
Applicants	54,500	53,500
Computer expenses	1,350	1,050
Equipment rental	27,500	25,000
Dues and subscriptions	2,200	2,100
Energy costs	22,100	20,900
Fertilizer	51,000	49,500
Gasoline and lubricants	20,500	19,900
Licenses and permits	650	650
Operating supplies	7,350	6,950
Professional development	3,500	3,420
Refuse removal	8,350	8,150
Repairs and maintenance		
Irrigation systems	4,500	4,350
Mowers, tractors, and trucks	45,300	44,200
Roads and paths	500	450
Sand and topsoil dressing	15,000	15,600
Seeds, flowers, and shrubs	4,200	3,200
Telephone	1,250	1,175
Uniforms	9,200	9,050
Vehicle expense	7,640	7,515
Total other expenses	286,590	276,660
TOTAL GOLF COURSE MAINTENANCE EXPENSES	$ 940,140	$ 905,560
CALCULATED COST PER HOLE	$ 52,230	$ 50,309

Racquet Sports—Schedule H
Years ended December 31, 20X2 and 20X1

	Period Ending	
	20X2	**20X1**
REVENUE		
Court fees	$ 4,950	$ 5,150
Rentals	380	420
Total revenue	5,330	5,570
DEPARTMENTAL EXPENSES		
Payroll and related expenses		
Salaries and wages	35,040	34,020
Payroll taxes and employee benefits	4,680	4,600
Employees' meals	1,400	1,350
Total payroll and related expenses	41,120	39,970
Other expenses		
Committee expense	6,300	4,300
Court maintenance	4,000	4,100
Dues and subscriptions	120	120
Laundry and linen	1,600	1,450
Gratis food	450	425
Professional development	250	200
Total other expenses	12,720	10,595
TOTAL DEPARTMENTAL EXPENSES	53,840	50,565
DEPARTMENTAL (LOSS)	$ (48,510)	$ (44,995)

Aquatic Sports—Schedule J

Years ended December 31, 20X2 and 20X1

		Period Ending	
		20X2	**20X1**
REVENUE			
Guest fees		$ 4,200	$ 3,900
Rentals		280	320
Total revenue		4,480	4,220
DEPARTMENTAL EXPENSES			
Payroll and related expenses			
Salaries and wages		15,250	15,000
Payroll taxes and employee benefits		5,400	5,400
Employees' meals		620	580
Total payroll and related expenses		21,270	20,980
Other expenses			
Equipment repairs and maintenance		2,000	1,500
Gratis food		450	425
Laundry and linen		4,880	3,060
Licenses and permits		180	180
Operating supplies		7,250	7,100
Prizes		1,200	1,200
Professional development		150	120
Uniforms		320	300
Other operating expenses		300	350
Total other expenses		16,730	14,235
TOTAL DEPARTMENTAL EXPENSES		38,000	35,215
DEPARTMENTAL (LOSS)		$ (33,520)	$ (30,995)

Locker Rooms—Schedule L
Years ended December 31, 20X2 and 20X1

	Period Ending	
	20X2	20X1
REVENUE		
Locker rentals	$ 97,800	$ 92,900
DEPARTMENTAL EXPENSES		
Payroll and related expenses		
Salaries and wages	69,700	67,700
Payroll taxes and employee benefits	9,145	9,040
Employees' meals	2,200	2,150
Total payroll and related expenses	81,045	78,890
Other expenses		
Gratis food	8,000	7,950
Laundry and linen	9,980	9,950
Member supplies	7,100	7,050
Operating supplies	4,200	4,000
Uniforms	400	380
Total other expenses	29,680	29,330
TOTAL DEPARTMENTAL EXPENSES	110,725	108,220
DEPARTMENTAL (LOSS)	$ (12,925)	$ (15,320)

Rentals and Other Revenue—Schedule O
Years ended December 31, 20X2 and 20X1

	Period Ending	
	20X2	20X1
REVENUE		
Space rentals and concessions	$ 2,400	$ 2,400
Cash discounts earned	150	130
Interest income	22,050	19,900
Member late fees	7,550	7,490
TOTAL RENTALS AND OTHER REVENUE	$ 32,150	$ 29,920

Administrative and General—Schedule P
Years ended December 31, 20X2 and 20X1

	Period Ending	
	20X2	**20X1**
DEPARTMENTAL EXPENSES		
Payroll and related expenses		
Salaries and wages	$ 405,000	$ 392,300
Payroll taxes and employee benefits	57,260	55,640
Employees' meals	4,400	4,250
Total payroll and related expenses	466,660	452,190
Other expenses		
Club publications	17,500	16,950
Computer expense	7,700	7,450
Credit card fees	770	690
Dues and subscriptions	6,500	6,350
Equipment rental and maintenance	3,180	3,180
Licenses and permits	4,100	3,950
Loss and damage	670	550
Postage	13,020	12,080
Printing and stationery	12,050	12,320
Professional development	3,500	3,350
Professional fees	20,850	19,500
Provision for doubtful accounts	10,200	8,500
Telephone	22,200	22,750
Trade associations and conferences	4,000	4,000
Vehicle expense	10,050	10,140
Website development and maintenance	7,500	2,400
Other operating expenses	7,450	7,380
Total other expenses	151,240	141,540
TOTAL ADMINISTRATIVE AND GENERAL EXPENSES	$ 617,900	$ 593,730

Facility Maintenance and Energy—Schedule R
Years ended December 31, 20X2 and 20X1

	20X2	20X1
DEPARTMENTAL EXPENSES		
Payroll and related expenses		
Salaries and wages	$ 216,000	$ 209,700
Payroll taxes and employee benefits	28,600	27,840
Employees' meals	4,110	4,090
Total payroll and related expenses	248,710	241,630
Other expenses		
Building	11,000	10,900
Dues and subscriptions	375	355
Electrical and mechanical equipment	11,250	10,350
Elevators	1,200	1,200
Floor coverings	5,100	5,050
Grounds and landscaping	14,500	18,230
HVAC	12,050	11,950
Painting and decorating	6,500	6,350
Plumbing	7,800	8,300
Professional development	450	450
Refuse removal	13,950	13,870
Uniforms	3,450	3,390
Vehicle expense	8,450	7,890
Other operating expenses	14,670	14,890
Total other expenses	110,745	113,175
TOTAL FACILITY MAINTENANCE EXPENSES	$ 359,455	$ 354,805
ENERGY COSTS		
Electricity	76,250	75,750
Fuel	33,500	33,110
Water	3,370	3,130
TOTAL ENERGY COSTS	$ 113,120	$ 111,990
TOTAL ENERGY AND FACILITY MAINTENANCE	$ 472,575	$ 466,795

Payroll, Payroll Taxes, and Benefits—Schedule U
Years ended December 31, 20X2 and 20X1

	SALARIES AND WAGES PERIOD ENDED		TAXES AND BENEFITS PERIOD ENDED		EMPLOYEE MEALS PERIOD ENDED	
	20X2	20X1	20X2	20X1	20X2	20X1
Food	$ 741,110	$ 727,425	$ 191,950	$ 188,300	$ 27,350	$ 26,700
Beverage	38,545	35,750	15,080	14,800	1,470	1,340
Entertainment	38,940	36,350	5,125	4,790	650	650
Overnight rooms	24,000	22,000	2,070	1,920	1,300	1,250
Golf operations	190,000	182,200	13,020	10,940	4,200	4,120
Golf course maintenance	575,300	551,750	71,850	70,900	6,400	6,250
Golf shop	36,000	33,000	2,950	2,700	1,300	1,380
Racquet sports	35,040	34,020	4,680	4,600	1,400	1,350
Aquatic sports	15,250	15,000	5,400	5,400	620	580
Locker rooms	69,700	67,700	9,145	9,040	2,200	2,150
Administrative and general	405,000	392,300	57,260	55,640	4,400	4,250
Facility maintenance and energy	216,000	209,700	28,600	27,840	4,110	4,090
Totals	$ 2,384,885	$ 2,307,195	$ 407,130	$ 396,870	$ 55,400	$ 54,110

Appendix F
Club Taxation

People frequently confuse the concepts of "tax-exempt," "not-for-profit," and "private." The terms are not interchangeable. They have distinct meanings with regard both to tax reporting and to financial reporting.

Because there already is an existing volume of literature addressing for-profit accounting, this publication focuses on the financial reporting of not-for-profit clubs. The term "not-for-profit" does not necessarily mean tax-exempt. Many clubs that are not-for-profit for GAAP purposes have never obtained federal tax-exempt status. Indeed, many clubs are required to be formed under the "not-for-profit" statutes of their particular state. To determine whether a club is a not-for-profit entity for financial reporting purposes, consider the definition from the May 2001 AICPA audit and accounting guide *Not-For-Profit Organizations*:

> An entity that possesses the following characteristics that distinguish it from a business enterprise: *(a)* contributions of significant amounts of resources from resource providers who do not expect commensurate or proportionate pecuniary return, *(b)* operating purposes other than to provide goods or services at a profit, and *(c)* absence of ownership interests like those of business enterprises.

The definition is extracted from SFAS No. 116. Included in the guide's list of organizations that meet the definition are "social and country clubs." Clubs may meet this definition because:

- many cannot provide a pecuniary return to members for their initiation fees due to private inurement rules and organizing documents;

- many formation documents state that the club is operating not for profit; and

- many cannot pay dividends to members, unlike a business, and often are incorporated as "non-stock" corporations, unlike most businesses.

The tax issues facing clubs are just as complex. However, all clubs need to consider some relatively simple club tax concepts as well.

Private Status

There are federal and state statutes that prohibit an invasion of a person's right to be left alone. The critical issue for clubs in the future may not be tax status, but rather private status. The more a club opens itself for outside business and the more it looks like a business, the more potential exists that a government agency or court will rule that the club is no longer private. A number of issues arise from this determination, including the ability to be selective in membership and the exemption from certain federal laws. Many states and localities already have enacted public accommodations legislation that restricts the rights of clubs. Use of club facilities by nonmembers, regardless of the percentage of use it constitutes, should be a concern for clubs wishing to maintain private status. A happy medium must be reached between the revenue provided from nonmembers and the potential cost of being treated as a public accommodation. This is the cost of exclusivity.

Taxable or Tax-Exempt?

Clubs fall into one of two primary categories: "regular businesses" and "membership organizations." "Regular businesses" include municipal golf courses, clubs owned by one or a number of investors, and developer-owned clubs. The tax rules that apply to every other "regular business" will apply to these clubs.

"Membership organizations" are those where the ownership is in the hands of the club members. These organizations have a special set of rules. Most often, these clubs have been organized in their state as a not-for-profit corporation. As stated above, this is not to be confused with tax-exempt. These not-for-profit clubs themselves then fall into two categories: those that have applied for tax-exempt status with the Internal Revenue Service under Section 501(c)(7) of the Internal Revenue Code (IRC) and those that have not made this application. Clubs that have not applied for tax-exempt status are, by default, subject to IRC Section 277 and are referred to as "277 taxable" clubs. The prime difference between "277 taxable" and "501(c)(7) tax-exempt" clubs is that member-related net profit will *never* be taxable to a 501(c)(7) tax-exempt club, while member-related net profit *could* be taxable to a 277 taxable club. Both membership organizations could owe income tax on nonmember net profit and net investment income.

Three-Column Approach

Membership organization clubs, whether they are tax-exempt under Section 501(c)(7) or taxable under Section 277 of the IRC, must record income and expenses in one of three categories. Think of this requirement in a three-column approach as noted below.

(1) Member Income and Expenses	(2) Nonmember Income and Expenses	(3) Investment Income and Expenses

All income from members related to using the club facilities and services will be recorded in the member column, while income received from nonmembers is recorded in the second column. The third column is where investment income is to be recorded. Expenses are recorded in their respective columns based upon one of a number of alternative accounting methods selected by the club—presumably the method that results in the lowest possible tax liability.

Only these three columns are necessary to master the basics of the accounting for tax purposes. Mastering exactly what income and expense is recorded in each column, and how net income or losses can be used to offset one another, is much more complicated. This requires more study and analysis of rules and regulations.

Member vs. Nonmember vs. Investment Income

For tax purposes, member, nonmember, and investment income must be differentiated. In the simplest of terms, "member income" generally is received from a person on the membership roster of the club. It will include the spouse and children of a member if only one name is recorded with the club. The IRS has taken the position that member income does *not* include income from a member for products and services of the club that are consumed off club premises. For example, the sale of Thanksgiving turkeys and holiday platters to be consumed at a member's home would be deemed to be "nontraditional" income and recorded as nonmember income.

"Nonmember income" is a catchall category for income from sources that are not member-related or investment income.

"Investment income" is income from investing club funds, such as interest on a bank account, dividends and capital gains from stock investments, and rental income (if the asset being rented is investment property). Fees charged to members for late payment of dues or installment payments on assessments should be classified as member income, not investment income.

The IRS has issued a number of rulings that will assist in the analysis of member vs. nonmember income of a club. One of these rulings, Revenue Procedure 71-17, stands out as a document that membership organizations need to read and understand. Issued in 1971, this Procedure can help both 277 taxable and 501(c)(7) tax-exempt clubs to identify what is member and nonmember income when nonmembers are in a group. A summary of the rule follows.

Summary of Revenue Procedure 71-17

Revenue Procedure 71-17 sets forth guidelines for determining the effect gross receipts derived from use of a social club's facilities by the general public have on the club's exemption from federal income tax under section 501(c)(7) of the IRC. The guidelines will be used in connection with the examination of annual returns on Forms 990 and 990-T filed by social clubs. The Revenue Procedure also describes the records required when nonmembers use a club's facilities and the circumstances under which a host-guest relationship will be assumed, which are relevant both for purposes of determining adherence to the exemption requirements and for computing (member) exempt function income. While the Revenue Procedure applies only to tax-exempt clubs, the IRS has extended certain of its requirements to 277 taxable clubs.

Use of a club's facilities by the general public (nonmembers) is significant for two reasons. It may indicate the existence of a nonexempt purpose of a 501(c)(7) tax-exempt club. Additionally, if not of sufficient substantiality to result in loss of 501(c)(7) tax exemption, it may make the club liable for income tax on nonmember income. The term "general public" as used in the Revenue Procedure means persons other than members of a club or their dependents or guests.

Minimum gross receipts standard for 501(c)(7) tax-exemption. A significant factor reflecting the existence of a nonexempt purpose of a 501(c)(7) membership organization is the amount of gross receipts derived from use of a club's facilities by the general public. The IRS will not rely on this factor alone as an audit standard if annual gross receipts from the general public for such use are $2,500 or less. When the amount is more than $2,500:

- If the organization receives 35 percent of its gross receipts from investments, then the organization may maintain its exemption under section 501(c)(7) of the IRC.

- If the organization receives no more than 15 percent of its gross receipts from nonmember use of club facilities and/or services, then the organization may maintain its exemption under section 501(c)(7).

- If the organization receives 35 percent of its gross receipts from outside its membership and no more than 15 percent of its gross receipts are derived from nonmember use of club facilities, then the organization may maintain its exemption under IRC 501(c)(7).

- If the organization exceeds the 35 and/or 15 percent limitations, then the organization may maintain its exempt status if it can show through facts and circumstances that "substantially all" of its activities are for "pleasure, recreation, and other nonprofitable purposes."

This minimum gross receipts standard reflects the audit experience of the IRS that gross receipts at or below this level do not, standing alone, usually demonstrate a nonexempt purpose. Even if gross receipts from the general public exceed this standard, it does not necessarily establish that there is a nonexempt purpose. A conclusion that there is a nonexempt purpose will be based on all the facts and circumstances, including but not limited to the gross receipts factor. This audit standard relates only to determinations of exempt status. There is no minimum audit tolerance with respect to unrelated business taxable income.

Assumption as to status of nonmembers that can be used by both 501(c)(7) and 277 taxable clubs. The determination of unrelated business income (UBI) for a tax-exempt club is different than for any other tax-exempt entity. For most tax-exempt entities, unless income is specifically stated to be unrelated business income, it is tax-exempt. A 501(c)(7) club is just the opposite. All income is considered nonmember income (and thus UBI) unless an exception is specifically stated. Member income is one exception. However, because of the structure of this section, the club is left with the burden of proof to show that income is member income. Failure to keep required records could result in the IRS claiming that an excessive amount of income is nonmember income. To reduce the burden, the procedure provides certain safe harbors:

1. Where a group of eight or fewer individuals, at least one of whom is a member, uses club facilities, it will be assumed for audit purposes that the nonmembers are the guests of the member, provided the club receives payment for such use directly from the member or the member's employer.

2. Where 75 percent or more of a group using club facilities are members, it will likewise be assumed for audit purposes that the nonmembers in the group are

guests of members, provided the club receives payment for such use directly from one or more of the members or the members' employers.

3. Payment by a member's employer will be assumed to be for a use that serves a direct business objective of the employee-member.

4. In all other situations, a host-guest relationship will not be assumed but must be substantiated. See below for the records required.

Recordkeeping requirements. With respect to parties of eight or fewer, the club need not maintain the records specified below. However, the club must maintain adequate records to substantiate that the group comprised eight or fewer individuals, that at least one of them was a member, and that the club received payment directly from members or their employers. Where the member makes payment directly to the club, the club is under no obligation to inquire about reimbursement.

With respect to the 75 percent-or-more rule, the club must maintain adequate records to substantiate that 75 percent or more of the persons in the group were, in fact, members of the club at the time of such use and that the club received payment directly from members or their employers. Where the member makes payment directly to the club, the club is under no obligation to inquire about reimbursement.

With respect to all other occasions involving use by nonmembers, the club must maintain books and records of each such use and the amount derived. This requirement applies even though the member pays initially for such use. This is an all-or-nothing determination. A function is either 100 percent member or nonmember, regardless of the number of each category in attendance.

In each instance, the record must contain the following information:

1. The date;

2. The total number in the party;

3. The number of nonmembers in the party;

4. The total charges;

5. The charges attributable to nonmembers;

6. The charges paid by nonmembers;

7. Where a member pays all or part of the charges attributable to nonmembers, a statement signed by the member indicating whether he or she has been or will be reimbursed for such nonmember use and, if so, the amount of the reimbursement.

Where the member's employer reimburses the member or makes direct payment to the club for the charges attributable to nonmembers, a statement signed by the member indicating the name of the employer; the amount of the payment attributable to the nonmember use; the nonmember's name and business or other relationship to the member; and the business, personal, or social purpose of the member served by the nonmember use must be provided. (The use of club facilities must serve some personal or social purpose of the employee-member or some direct business objective of the employee-member; the mere use of club facilities for the accommodation *of the member's employer* does not serve a business, personal, or social purpose of the *member*.) If a large number of nonmembers are involved and they are readily identifiable as a particular class of individuals, the member may record such class, rather than all of the names.

Where a nonmember other than the employer of the member makes payment to the club or reimburses a member and a claim is made that the amount was paid gratuitously for the benefit of a member, a statement signed by the member indicating the donor's name and relationship to the member and containing information to substantiate the gratuitous nature of the payment or reimbursement must be provided.

Failure to maintain such records or make them available to the IRS for examination will preclude use of the minimum gross receipts standard and audit assumptions set forth in the Revenue Procedure. Both 501(c)(7) tax-exempt and 277 taxable clubs must comply with the various rules set forth by the IRS.

Other Issues

Sale of Property

The IRS continues its aggressive attack on the deferral of gain by a 501(c)(7) tax-exempt club when it sells property used in its exempt function. If property used directly in a club's exempt function is sold by the organization, and other property is purchased and used directly in the performance of its exempt function within a period beginning one year before the date of the sale and ending three years after the sale date, the gain is recognized only to the extent that the organization's sale price of the old property exceeds the cost of purchasing the new property.

Determining whether property is used directly in the exempt function of a club has been a source of controversy with the IRS over the years. The Service's definition continues to shrink as it challenges more clubs on the deferral. At the end of 2000, the IRS issued a private letter ruling addressing the issue again. Among a club's assets was a painting received by bequest in 1933. The painting hung in the dining room. The club contended that the painting was an integral part of its exempt function because it enhanced a room where the exempt activities take place. The club is not in the business of selling art and is not an investor in artwork. The club has not sold any other artwork. The club sold the painting to an unrelated third party and plans to use the proceeds in the furtherance of its exempt purpose. The IRS found that the painting was used in the club's exempt purpose.

While the decision is correct, the disturbing point is the extent that the letter ruling went into the history of the painting and the fact that the club was not a trader in artwork. Based on the decision in *Atlanta Athletic Club*, the IRS should not look at the intent of the parties, but rather what was done with the painting. It was used in the club's exempt function. This should have been the end of the story. Expect the IRS to continue its examination of clubs when the issue of a deferral of gain is raised.

Reciprocal Income

To provide benefits to its members, a club may enter into a reciprocal arrangement with other clubs around the corner or around the world. The arrangements allow the member to use the facilities of another club because of its relationship with the member's home club. The IRS has considered the income generated by such activities as nonmember income. As such, it is subject to the 15 percent limit on nonmember use of club facilities.

Questions have been raised as to whether this income is truly nonmember. Unfortunately, the position of the IRS is clear. In a 1979 ruling, the IRS stated:

> A guest of a nonprofit social club is an individual who is a guest of a member of the club and who ordinarily does not reimburse the member for the guest's expenses. On the other hand, *amounts paid to a social club by visiting members of another social club are amounts paid by nonmembers,* even though both clubs are of like nature and the amounts paid are for goods, facilities, or services provided by such a social club under a reciprocal arrangement with such other social club.

This position was restated in a general council memorandum in 1984. Unless the Service issues guidance reversing this position, a club would be wise to follow existing precedent.

Disclosure Rules

An organization must make available for public inspection or copying without charge (other than a reasonable charge for copying) its application for tax-exempt status and its three most recent annual returns. "Reasonable" is defined as no more than the IRS charges for its copies—currently, $1 for the first page and 15 cents per page thereafter.

An application includes Form 1023 or Form 1024, plus all required documents and statements, as well as documents issued by the IRS. These would include a favorable determination letter or list of IRS questions about the application. Exceptions from the disclosure requirements include an application from an entity not yet recognized as tax-exempt; an exemption application filed before July 15, 1987, unless the organization had a copy of the application on that date; and material, including adverse determination letters, that is not subject to disclosure such as trade secrets, copyrights, etc.

The return that must be disclosed is an exact copy of what is filed with the IRS, including all attachments and schedules. Particular mention is made of Schedule A and the parts of the return that show compensation paid to specific individuals. Form 990-T, returns filed more than three years before the date of the request, and the name and address of any contributor need not be disclosed.

Generally, in-person requests for copies must be provided the same day. The organization does not have to respond to oral requests over the telephone. However, it does need to respond to requests made by regular mail, e-mail, telefax, or private delivery service. It has 30 days in which to respond in these instances. Requests for copies of less than the entire return (e.g., salary information only) must be honored.

Two major exceptions to the requirements exist. First, if the documents are available on an accessible Internet site *and* the organization informs people requesting copies of the Internet address *and* the document can be downloaded and printed so that the final product is the same as that filed with the IRS, then no additional disclosure is required. Second, if the IRS district director determines that the organization is subject to a harassment campaign involving document requests, and the specific request is part of the campaign, then disclosure is not required. Note that the organization must make a request for ruling to the IRS that it is being harassed.

While long and detailed, the regulations appear to represent a reasonable approach to the new disclosure requirements. However, it is important to establish one contact person to ensure that the rules are followed and that those requesting the information are known.

Corporate Membership

Recently, questions have been raised concerning the solicitation of corporate memberships by 501(c)(7) tax-exempt clubs. It is important that clubs know the rules before developing a corporate membership program. The IRS has ruled that tax-exempt clubs may *not* have corporate members. Its position is that artificial entities are incapable of producing the personal contacts and fellowships contemplated in a tax-exempt social club. Any income from a corporate membership will be treated as unrelated business income.

These rules do not apply to tax-exempt clubs that allow *corporation-sponsored* members. The IRS has held that corporations, partnerships, or other business entities may sponsor a member in a club—in effect, a representative designated by the business. No membership problem arises if the individual is subject to the same approval procedure by the membership committee as is every other member. It is the individual, not the business, who is the member and has all the rights and responsibilities.

Advertising

Advertising continues to be a problem for clubs. Many issues have been raised concerning whether clubs can advertise for potential new members or for non-member use of club facilities. While not specifically prohibited for tax purposes, it may be unwise because of the impact on private status.

But what about businesses that want to advertise with the club? Is it allowable to have members or even nonmembers advertise in a club newsletter or directory, and what are the tax implications? Advertising in club publications is allowed. If done by nonmembers, it is unrelated business income. If done by members, questions arise as to its proper classification. An issue arises as to whether a social club can offset its advertising income with excess readership costs. The IRS is against it, but the Tax Court took a contrary view. The Court held that an exempt social club may deduct expenses attributable to its publication of a periodical in computing its unrelated business taxable income. The Court threw out all of the IRS's arguments, and told the Service to change its regulations if it wanted to get its proposed result.

Appendix G
Expense Dictionary

INTRODUCTION

This dictionary is designed to help members of the club industry classify, in accordance with the *Uniform System of Financial Reporting for Clubs*, the numerous expense and payroll-related items encountered in their daily work. It will serve as a ready reference for Board members, managers, and purchasing agents, showing them to which account or expense group each expense item will be charged.

It should be noted, however, that not all property expenditures are recorded as expenses. A material expenditure made to purchase an item with a useful life of more than one year typically will be capitalized. That is, the amount will be included as an asset on the statement of financial position and expensed through depreciation or amortization over the item's useful life. Materiality is an important element of the decision to capitalize or expense a purchase. An inexpensive item may have a useful life of more than one year. While this useful life would dictate that the item be capitalized, the benefit of capitalizing the item may not outweigh the cost of setting up and maintaining the depreciation records. Consequently, the item may be expensed. The dollar amount that determines whether an item will be capitalized or expensed is a matter of judgment. Once the amount is established, it should become part of club policy and be followed consistently.

Some expenditures extend the life of an asset or add value to an asset. Generally accepted accounting principles require that these expenditures be capitalized and depreciated over the estimated remaining useful life of the asset. The most common example is an expenditure to repair property and equipment. If the repair expenditure only restores the value of the asset to its condition before the repair, the expenditure should be expensed. However, if the expenditure extends the life of the asset or increases the value of the asset, the expenditure should be capitalized.

Finally, there are expenditures that are normally expensed, but that, under certain circumstances, are more properly capitalized. Examples include interest costs incurred during the development, construction, or renovation of a club and software development costs associated with the purchase of a new computer system. While interest costs and software costs may be expensed in some situations, generally accepted accounting principles prescribe that, when these expenditures are incurred as part of the acquisition of an asset, it is proper to include these expenditures in the total amount that is capitalized. Each club's controller should be familiar with the guidelines established by the appropriate accounting principle for the treatment of these and other similar expenditures.

How to Read the Expense Dictionary

GUIDE TO ABBREVIATIONS	
Abbreviation	Department/Function/Item
A&G.	Administrative and General
China.	China, Glassware, and Silver
Depr. & Amort.	Depreciation and Amortization
Elec. & Mech.	Electrical and Mechanical Equipment
FC&IT	Fixed Charges and Income Taxes
FF&E	Furniture, Fixtures, and Equipment
FM&E	Facility Maintenance and Energy
OOD	Other Operating Departments
PT&EB	Payroll Taxes and Employee Benefits

The Expense Dictionary is divided into two columns. Column I lists expense items alphabetically. Column II identifies the accounts to which the expense items would be charged. Items purchased for direct sale in any department are not included, since their distribution is obviously direct to the cost of sales of the department concerned.

Column II lists expense accounts in a number of ways. The following is a short explanation of the various forms these listings can take.

If a department, operational function, or cost center is followed by a dash, the entry following the dash is the account or line item charged within that department, operational function, or cost center. For example, the entry for **Accountants' Fees** is **A&G—Professional Fees**.

If more than one department or cost center can charge a particular expense item to accounts or line items with the same name, the departments or cost centers are separated by diagonal slashes. For example, the entry for **Curtains—Shower** is **Locker Rooms/Overnight Rooms—Laundry & Linen**.

If the same item is charged by different departments or cost centers to different accounts or line items, departments and accounts are listed consecutively and separated by semicolons. For example, the entry for **Books** is **Overnight Rooms— Member & Guest Supplies; Clubhouse—Library**.

Some expenses are broken down even further. For example, the entry for **Amortization—Mortgage Expense** is **FC&IT—Interest Expense—Mortgage Payable**. Fixed Charges and Income Taxes is the schedule, Interest Expense is the subsection, and Mortgage Payable is the line item.

Note that Column II is designed to identify *line items* on one or more statements or schedules. It does *not* attempt to list or detail the sub-accounts (if any) that may "roll up" into the line item. Depending on a club's individual needs, any given line item on a statement or schedule may be either an individual account or a grouping of accounts. When a club wishes to classify its expenses in greater detail than is shown here, it may further assign its expenses into any relevant sub-accounts. For example, the entry for **Beverage Spoons** is **Beverage—Operating Supplies**. If it chooses, a club might set up a sub-account called "Utensils" as one of several sub-accounts (including such things as Menus, Paper Supplies, and Cleaning Supplies) that would be combined and listed as a single total under Operating Supplies on the Beverage schedule.

Many of the items defined here could easily be further sorted into more specific accounts as identified in the Sample Chart of Accounts in Appendix D. This expense dictionary is intended simply to get the user to the proper line item on the proper statement or schedule.

Expense Dictionary

Item	Classification
A	
Accountants' Fees	A&G—Professional Fees
Acids	Overnight Rooms/Clubhouse/Aquatic Sports/House Laundry—Operating Supplies
Adding Machine Tapes	All Departments—Operating Supplies
Advertising—Classified	All Departments— Other Operating Expenses
Air-Cooling Systems Repairs	FM&E—HVAC
Alarm Service—Fire or Burglar	Clubhouse—Security
Amenities—Locker and Rooms	Overnight Rooms—Member & Guest Supplies; Locker Rooms—Member Supplies
Amortization—Leasehold Improvements	FC&IT—Depr. & Amort.—Leaseholds & Leasehold Improvements
Amortization—Mortgage Expense	FC&IT—Interest Expense—Mortgage Payable
Answering Machines	All Departments—Telephone
Armored Car Service	A&G—Contract Services
Ash Trays	Overnight Rooms/Food/Beverage—China
Association Dues	All Departments—Dues & Subscriptions
Athletic Equipment for Employees	All Departments—Other Operating Expenses
Attorney's Fees—For Collections	A&G—Credit & Collection Expenses
Attorney's Fees—Other Than Collections	A&G—Professional Fees
Audit Fees—Public Accountants	A&G—Professional Fees
Auto Rental	Various Departments—Vehicle Expense
Auto/Truck Repair and Supplies— Used by Property	Various Departments—Vehicle Expense
Awards—Employees	All Departments—Other Operating Expenses
Awnings—Cleaning	FM&E—Building
B	
Bad Debts	A&G—Provision for Doubtful Accounts

Item	Classification
Bag Check Supplies	Overnight Rooms/Golf Ops.—Printing & Stationery
Bags (Laundry)	All Departments—Laundry & Linen
Bags (Retail Outlet)	All Departments—Operating Supplies
Balls—Sports (Golf, Racquets, Other)	Golf Ops./Racquet Sports/OOD—Operating Supplies
Balls—Range	Golf Ops.—Driving Range
Bank Checks, Charges	A&G—Bank Charges
Bank Exchange on Checks and Currency	A&G—Bank Charges
Banquet Reports	Food/Beverage—Printing & Stationery
Bar Appetizers/Snacks	Beverage—Gratis Food
Bar Utensils	Beverage—Operating Supplies
Basket Liners, Waste Paper	Food/Beverage/Overnight Rooms/Clubhouse—Operating Supplies
Bath Mats	Overnight Rooms—Laundry & Linen
Bathing Caps	Aquatic Sports—Operating Supplies
Batteries—Transistor	FM&E—Operating Supplies
Batteries—Cart	Golf Ops.—Golf Cart Batteries
Bedspreads	Overnight Rooms—Laundry & Linen
Bedspreads—Cleaning	Overnight Rooms—Laundry & Linen
Beeper Rental	All Departments—Equipment Rental
Beverage Licenses	Beverage—Licenses & Permits
Beverage Spoons	Beverage—Operating Supplies
Beverage Stirrers—Glass	Beverage—Operating Supplies
Billing Statements/Invoices	A&G—Printing & Stationery
Binders and Binding System Accessories	All Departments—Operating Supplies
Blankets	Overnight Rooms—Laundry & Linen
Blankets—Cleaning	Overnight Rooms—Laundry & Linen
Boiler Inspection (Contractors)	FM&E—Elec. & Mech.
Boiler Repairs	FM&E—Elec. & Mech.
Books	Overnight Rooms—Member & Guest Supplies; Clubhouse—Library
Bottle Openers (Loose)	Food/Beverage—Operating Supplies
Bowls	Food—China
Bread and Butter Plates	Food—China
Bridge (Cards) Supplies	Clubhouse—Member Supplies
Brochures	A&G—Other Operating Expenses
Brooms	All Departments—Operating Supplies
Brushes—Cleaning	All Departments—Operating Supplies
Brushes—Hair	Overnight Rooms—Member & Guest Supplies; Locker Rooms—Member Supplies
Building and Contents Insurance	FC&IT—Insurance—Building & Contents
Building Repairs	FM&E—Building
Bulletin Board Supplies	Clubhouse—Operating Supplies
Bulletin (Newsletter)	A&G—Club Publications
Burglar Alarm Service	Clubhouse—Security
Business Cards	A&G—Printing & Stationery

Item	Classification

C

Item	Classification
Cable TV	Overnight Rooms—Cable/Satellite Television; Entertainment/Clubhouse—Other Operating Expenses
Calculators	A&G—Operating Supplies & Equipment
Calendars and Diaries	A&G—Operating Supplies & Equipment
Candles	Food/Beverage/Overnight Rooms—Operating Supplies—Other
Candy	Overnight Rooms—Member & Guest Supplies; Clubhouse/Locker Rooms—Member Supplies; Food/Beverage—Operating Supplies
Carafes	Food/Beverage/Overnight Rooms—China
Carfares, Taxis	All Departments—Other Operating Expenses
Carpet Repairs	FM&E—Floor Coverings
Carpet Sweepers	Clubhouse/Overnight Rooms/Food/Beverage—Operating Supplies
Carts—Golf Club–Owned	Assets—Vehicles
Carts—Leased (Operating Lease)	Golf Ops.—Cart Rentals
Carts—Rental—Tournament Event	Golf Ops.—Tournament Expenses
Cart Maintenance (Parts)	Golf Ops.—Golf Cart Repairs & Maintenance
Cash Boxes	A&G—Operating Supplies & Equipment
Cashier Supplies	A&G—Operating Supplies & Equipment
Casual Labor (Temporary Help)	All Departments—Salaries & Wages
Charge Envelopes/Forms/Vouchers	All Departments—Printing & Stationery
Checks—Bank	A&G—Printing & Stationery
Chemicals—Fire Extinguisher	FM&E—Operating Supplies
Chemicals—Laundry	House Laundry—Laundry Supplies
China—F&B Use	Food/Beverage—China
Chits	All Departments—Printing & Stationery
Christmas	See Holiday
Classified Ads	All Departments—Other Operating Expenses
Cleaning Compounds and Supplies	All Departments—Operating Supplies
Clinic—Employees	All Departments—PT&EB
Clipboards	A&G—Operating Supplies & Equipment; All Other Departments—Operating Supplies
Cocktail Napkins—Paper	Food/Beverage—Operating Supplies
Coffee Bags	Food/Beverage—Operating Supplies
Coffee (Free)	Food/Beverage/Overnight Rooms—Gratis Food
Coffee Pots	Food/Beverage/Overnight Rooms—China

Item	Classification
Coffee Urn Repairs	Food—Equipment Repair & Maintenance
Coin/Currency Equipment and Supplies	A&G—Operating Supplies & Equipment
Collection Fees	A&G—Credit & Collection Expenses
Combs	Overnight Rooms—Member & Guest Supplies; Locker Rooms—Member Supplies
Commissions—Credit Card Charge	A&G—Credit Card Fees
Commissions—Employees	All Departments—Salaries & Wages
Complimentary Beverage	Beverage—Gratis Food
Complimentary Food	Food—Gratis Food
Complimentary Rooms—Musicians and Entertainers	Food/Beverage—Music & Entertainment; Entertainment—Contract Entertainment
Compotes	Food/Beverage—China
Computer Forms; Manuals; Supplies	All Departments—Computer Expense
Computer Software—Commercial Applications	All Departments—Computer Expense
Consultant Fees, Professional	A&G—Professional Fees; Various Departments—Contract Services
Containers—Liquid, Paper	Food/Beverage—Operating Supplies
Contract Cleaning	Various—Contract Services
Contract Cleaning—Fumigation	Various Departments—Contract Services
Contract Entertainment	Food/Beverage—Music & Entertainment; Entertainment—Contract Entertainment; Clubhouse—Other Operating Expenses
Contract Exterminating	Food/Beverage—Contract Services; FM&E—Pest Control
Contributions	A&G—Donations
Cooking Utensils	Food/Beverage—Operating Supplies
Copier Paper	All Departments—Printing & Stationery
Copier—Rental/Operating Lease	All Departments—Equipment Rental
Copier Supplies	All Departments—Printing & Stationery
Copying Service	All Departments—Printing & Stationery
Copyright Licenses	Food/Beverage—Licenses & Permits
Corkscrews	Beverage—Operating Supplies
Corsages	Food/Beverage—Operating Supplies; Clubhouse—Member Supplies; Overnight Rooms—Member & Guest Supplies
Court Fees	A&G—Professional Fees
Credit Card Commissions	A&G—Credit Card Fees
Credit and Collection Expenses	A&G—Credit & Collection Expenses
Cups—Bouillon, Coffee, Custard, Tea	Food/Beverage—China
Cups—Paper	Food/Beverage/Locker Rooms—Operating Supplies
Cups (Greens)	Golf Course Maint.—Operating Supplies
Curtain Cleaning	FM&E—Curtains & Draperies; All Other Departments—Laundry & Linen

Item	Classification
Curtains—Shower	Locker Rooms/Overnight Rooms—Laundry & Linen

D

Item	Classification
Damaged Articles—Member or Guest	All Departments—Other Operating Expenses
Data Supplies and Accessories	All Departments—Computer Expense
Data Processing Expenses	All Departments—Computer Expense
Decorations	Entertainment—Decorations & Props; Clubhouse—Plants & Decorations; All Other Departments—Other Operating Expenses
Deodorants	Locker Rooms—Member Supplies; Overnight Rooms—Member & Guest Supplies
Depreciation—Building	FC&IT—Depr. & Amort.—Building & Improvements
Depreciation—Equipment	FC&IT—Depr. & Amort.—FF&E
Desk Accessories (Employee)	A&G—Operating Supplies & Equipment; All Other Departments—Operating Supplies
Desk Accessories—Rooms	Overnight Rooms—Member & Guest Supplies
Detective Service	Clubhouse—Security
Detergents	Clubhouse/Food/Beverage—Operating Supplies; House Laundry—Laundry Supplies
Direct Mail Expenses—Outside Service	A&G—Other Operating Expenses
Directional Signs (Inside Building)	Clubhouse—Other Operating Expenses
Directories	All Departments—Printing & Stationery
Directors' Expense	A&G—Directors & Committees
Dishes	Food/Beverage—China
Dishwasher Repairs	Food—Equipment Repair & Maintenance
Dishwashing Compounds	Food/Beverage—Operating Supplies
Disinfectants	Locker Rooms/Clubhouse/Overnight Rooms/Food/Beverage—Operating Supplies
Disks (Computer)	All Departments—Computer Expense
Divot Mix and Supplies	Golf Course Maint.—Operating Supplies
Doilies	Food/Beverage—Operating Supplies
Donations	A&G—Donations
Doubtful Accounts—Provision for	A&G—Provision for Doubtful Accounts
Drapery Cleaning	FM&E—Curtains & Draperies; All Other Departments—Laundry & Linen
Drinking Glasses	Food/Beverage/Overnight Rooms—China
Drugs and Other Medical Supplies—Employees	All Departments—PT&EB
Dues—Association	All Departments—Dues & Subscriptions

Item	Classification
Dust Cloths	Clubhouse/Overnight Rooms—Operating Supplies

E

Item	Classification
Educational Activities/Supplies . . . . for Employees	All Departments—Professional Development
Electric Bulbs	FM&E—Operating Supplies
Elevator Repairs	FM&E—Elevators
Employee Credit Union	All Departments—PT&EB
Employee Housing/Lodging	All Departments—PT&EB
Employee Investigations	All Departments—Other Operating Expenses
Employee Meals	All Departments—Employees' Meals
Employee Relations Expense	All Departments—PT&EB
Employee Transportation	All Departments—Other Operating Expenses
Employment Agency Fees	All Departments—Other Operating Expenses
Engineering Supplies	FM&E—Operating Supplies
Engraving and Lettering	Clubhouse—Other Operating Expenses
Entertainment and Music	Food/Beverage—Music & Entertainment; Entertainment—Contract Entertainment
Envelopes—Member Use	Overnight Rooms—Member & Guest Supplies; Clubhouse—Member Supplies
Envelopes—Club Use	All Departments—Printing & Stationery
Exchange on Bank Checks and Currency . .	A&G—Bank Charges
Express Delivery Charges	A&G—Postage; All Other Departments—Other Operating Expenses
Extension Cords	FM&E—Operating Supplies

F

Item	Classification
Face Cloths—Member	Locker Rooms/Overnight Rooms—Laundry & Linen
Facial Tissues—Member	Clubhouse/Locker Rooms—Member Supplies; Overnight Rooms—Member & Guest Supplies
Favors	Clubhouse/Food/Beverage—Operating Supplies; Entertainment—Prizes
Fax Machine Supplies and Accessories	All Departments—Telephone
Federal Social Security Taxes	All Departments—PT&EB
Federal Unemployment Taxes (FUTA)	All Departments—PT&EB
Fertilizer	Golf Course Maint.—Fertilizer; FM&E—Grounds & Landscaping
Film Purchase and Developing	A&G—Club Publications; All Other Departments—Other Operating Expenses
Film Purchasing and Developing—Related to Website	A&G—Website Development & Maintenance

Item	Classification
Films	Entertainment—Films; Food/Beverage—Music & Entertainment
Fines	A&G—Other Operating Expenses
Fitness Equipment—Asset	Assets—FF&E
Fitness Instructor—Contract	Health & Fitness—Contract Services
Fitness Instructor—Employee	Health & Fitness—Salaries & Wages
Fitness Supplies	Health & Fitness—Athletic Supplies
Fire Alarm Service	Clubhouse—Security
Fire Extinguisher Chemicals	FM&E—Operating Supplies
Firewood	Clubhouse—Operating Supplies
First Aid Supplies	All Departments—Other Operating Expenses
Flags—Golf	Golf Course Maint.—Operating Supplies
Flatware	Food/Beverage—China
Floor Plans	Overnight Rooms—Printing & Stationery
Floor Wax	Clubhouse/Overnight Rooms/FM&E—Operating Supplies
Flowers	Clubhouse—Plants & Decorations; Food/Beverage—Other Operating Expenses
Foil Wrapping	Food/Beverage—Operating Supplies
Folios	Overnight Rooms—Printing & Stationery
Food—Gratis	Various Departments—Gratis Food
Food Licenses	Food—Licenses & Permits
Forms—General and Printed	All Departments—Printing & Stationery
Forms—Computer (Pre-printed Checks; Statements)	All Departments—Computer Expense
Freight Charges	A&G—Postage; All Other Departments—Other Operating Expenses
Fruit Baskets/Gifts (Complimentary)	Overnight Rooms—Member & Guest Supplies
Fuel	FM&E—Fuel
Fuel—Kitchen	Food—Kitchen Fuel
Fumigators	Clubhouse/Food/Beverage/Locker Room/Overnight Rooms—Contract Services; FM&E—Pest Control
Furniture Polish	Clubhouse/Rooms/Food/Beverage—Operating Supplies
Furniture Rental	Food/Beverage/Clubhouse/Overnight Rooms—Equipment Rental
Furniture Repairs	FM&E—Furniture

G

Item	Classification
Garbage Removal	FM&E—Refuse Removal
Garment Bags	Overnight Rooms—Member & Guest Supplies
Gas—Cooking	Food—Kitchen Fuel
Gas—for Heating and Fuel	FM&E—Fuel

Item	Classification
Gasoline—Motor Vehicles (Company and Employee Use)	Various Departments—Vehicle Expense
Gasoline—Motor Vehicles (Member and Guest Transportation)	Various Departments—Other Operating Expenses
Glass Bowls/Dishes	Food/Beverage—China
Glass Pitchers	Food/Beverage/Overnight Rooms—China
Glassware	Food/Beverage/Overnight Rooms—China
Golf Supplies on the Golf Course (Flags, Markers, Cups, Towels)	Golf Course Maint.—Operating Supplies
Golf Carts	See Carts
Golf Towels—Member	Golf Ops.—Operating Supplies
Golf Spikes	Golf Ops./Locker Rooms—Operating Supplies
Golf Balls—Range	Golf Ops.—Driving Range
Gratis Food (Not Used in the Preparation of Mixed Drinks)	Various Departments—Gratis Food
Gratuities and Gifts (Other than Employees or Guests)	All Departments—Other Operating Expenses
Grounds Expense (Common Areas)	FM&E—Grounds & Landscaping

H

Item	Classification
Handicap Costs	Golf Ops.—Other Operating Expenses
Hangers.............................	Clubhouse/Locker Rooms—Member Supplies; Overnight Rooms—Member & Guest Supplies
Help Wanted Ads	All Departments—Other Operating Expenses
Holiday Fund—Member Contribution	Liabilities—Current Liabilities—Special Funds
Holiday Payroll—Funded by Member Contributions	All Departments—Salaries & Wages
Holiday Payroll—Hours Worked	All Departments—Salaries & Wages
Holiday Decorations and Flowers	Food/Beverage—Other Operating Expenses—Decorations; Clubhouse—Plants & Decorations
Hospitalization Insurance	All Departments—PT&EB
House Committee—Expenses	Clubhouse/Food/Beverage—Other Operating Expenses; A&G—Directors & Committees
Housekeeper and Attendants' Reports	Overnight Rooms—Printing & Stationery
Housing—Employees	All Departments—PT&EB

I

Item	Classification
Ice/Ice Buckets	Food/Beverage/Overnight Rooms—Operating Supplies
Insecticides	Golf Course Maint.—Applicants
Insurance—Building and Contents; Fire; General	FC&IT—Insurance—Building & Contents

Item	Classification
Insurance—Dental (Non-union)	All Departments—PT&EB
Insurance—Disability (Non-union)	All Departments—PT&EB
Insurance—Health (Non-union)	All Departments—PT&EB
Insurance Reimbursement—Employee Portion (Non-union)	All Departments—PT&EB
Insurance—Union	All Departments—PT&EB
Insurance—Liability	FC&IT—Insurance—Liability
Insurance—Life	All Departments—PT&EB
Insurance—Workers' Compensation	All Departments—PT&EB
Interest Expense	FC&IT—Interest Expense
Internal Audit Expense	A&G—Professional Fees
Internet—Hosting Fees	A&G—Website Development & Maintenance
Internet Connection Charges (DSL, T1, Modem, Cable, Wireless)	A&G/Clubhouse—Telephone; Telecommunications—Computer Expense
Interview Expense	All Departments—Other Operating Expenses
Investigation of Employees	All Departments—Other Operating Expenses

K

Item	Classification
Keyboards—Mouse	All Departments—Computer Expense
Kitchenette Expenses	Overnight Rooms—Member & Guest Supplies
Knives	Food/Beverage—Operating Supplies

L

Item	Classification
Ladles	Food/Beverage—Operating Supplies
Landscaping—Common Areas	FM&E—Grounds & Landscaping
Laser Printer Supplies and Accessories	All Departments—Computer Expense
Laundry—Outside Services	All Departments—Laundry & Linen
Laundry—In-house Supplies	House Laundry—Laundry Supplies; Overnight Rooms/Food/Beverage/ Health and Fitness/Locker Rooms/ Aquatic Sports—Laundry & Linen
Leased Employees (Temporary)	All Departments—Salaries & Wages
Leasehold Improvements Amortization ...	FC&IT—Depr. & Amort.—Leaseholds & Leasehold Improvements
Legal Fees and Expenses	A&G—Professional Fees
Letters for Bulletin/Sign Boards	A&G—Office Supplies & Equipment
Lettering for Wall Plaques	All Departments—Other Operating Expenses
Licenses and Permits—F&B	Food/Beverage—Licenses & Permits
Licenses—Equipment Operation	Food/Beverage/Golf Course Maint./ Aquatic Sports—Licenses & Permits; All Other Departments—Other Operating Expenses

Item	Classification
Licenses—Music (ASCAP, BMI)	Food/Beverage—Licenses & Permits; Entertainment—Royalties
Licenses and Permits—Property	Clubhouse—Licenses & Permits
Limousine	All Departments—Other Operating Expenses
Linens (All Types)	All Departments—Laundry & Linen
Linen Rental	Food/Beverage/Clubhouse/Overnight Rooms—Laundry & Linen
Literature—Educational for Employees	All Departments—Professional Development
Lobby Cleaning (on Contract)	Clubhouse—Contract Services
Lobby Signs	FM&E—Operating Supplies
Lock Repairs	FM&E—Elec. & Mech.
Locker Supplies—Amenities	Locker Rooms—Member Supplies
Locker Supplies—Cleaning	Locker Rooms—Operating Supplies
Locker Supplies—Paper	Locker Rooms—Operating Supplies
Lodging of Employees	All Departments—PT&EB
Log Books	A&G/Overnight Rooms/Food/Beverage—Printing & Stationery
Lost and Damaged Articles (Guest)	Clubhouse/Overnight Rooms/A&G—Other Operating Expenses
Lost and Found Reports	Clubhouse/Overnight Rooms—Printing & Stationery

M

Item	Classification
Magazines (Member and Guest)	Clubhouse—Newspapers & Periodicals; Overnight Rooms—Member & Guest Supplies
Magazines—Trade	All Departments—Dues & Subscriptions
Mailing Supplies	A&G— Printing & Stationery
Maintenance Contracts—Electric Signs	FM&E—Other Operating Expenses
Maintenance Contracts—Office Equipment	Most Departments—Contract Services
Management Fees	A&G—Professional Fees
Manuals—Educational or Training	All Departments—Professional Development
Markers (Yardage)	Golf Course Maint.—Operating Supplies
Marquee Licenses	A&G—Licenses & Permits
Matches	Food/Beverage—Operating Supplies; Overnight Rooms—Member & Guest Supplies
Mats—Bath	Overnight Rooms—Laundry & Linen
Mats—Floor or Rubber	FM&E—Floor Covering
Mattress Protectors	Overnight Rooms—Laundry & Linen
Meals—Employees	All Departments—Employees' Meals
Meals and Entertainment—Outside	A&G—Other Operating Expenses

Item	Classification
Mechanical Music	Food/Beverage—Music & Entertainment; Entertainment—Other Operating Expenses
Medical Fees/Supplies (Service to Employees)	All Departments —PT&EB
Membership Dues—Associations	All Departments—Dues & Subscriptions
Member Supplies	Locker Rooms/Clubhouse—Member Supplies; Overnight Rooms—Member & Guest Supplies
Menus	Food/Beverage—Operating Supplies
Message Envelopes (Telephone)	Clubhouse/A&G/Telecommunications—Printing & Stationery
Metal Polish	Overnight Rooms/Food/Beverage—Operating Supplies
Mixing Bowls and Spoons	Food—Operating Supplies
Mops and Mop Handles and Wringers	All Departments—Operating Supplies
Mortgage Interest	FC&IT—Interest Expense—Mortgage Payable
Motor Repairs—General Equipment	FM&E—Elec. & Mech.
Motor Repairs—Golf Course Equipment ...	Golf Course Maint.—Repairs & Maintenance—Mowers, Tractors & Trucks
Mouse (Computer)	All Departments—Computer Expense
Mouse Traps	FM&E—Pest Control
Mouthwash	Locker Rooms—Member Supplies; Overnight Rooms—Member & Guest Supplies
Municipal Taxes—Beverages	Beverage—Licenses & Permits
Music and Musicians	Food/Beverage—Music & Entertainment; Entertainment—Contract Entertainment
Music Licenses	Food/Beverage—Licenses & Permits; Entertainment—Licenses & Permits/Royalties

N

Item	Classification
Name Badges	All Departments—Uniforms
Napkins—Linen	Food/Beverage—Laundry & Linen
Napkins—Paper	Food/Beverage—Operating Supplies
Needle and Thread	Locker Rooms—Member Supplies; Overnight Rooms—Member & Guest Supplies; Food/Beverage—Operating Supplies
Nets and Tapes	Racquet Sports—Operating Supplies
Newspapers—Guest Use (Rooms)	Overnight Rooms—Member & Guest Supplies
Newspapers—Lobby and Member Use	Clubhouse—Newspapers & Periodicals
Notary Fees	A&G—License & Permits
Notary Fees—Collection of Accounts	A&G—Credit & Collection Expenses

Item	Classification
Notebooks—Board	A&G—Directors & Committees
Notebooks—Committees	A&G—Directors & Committees
Notebooks—Document Storage	A&G—Other Operating Expenses

O

Item	Classification
Oil—Heating	FM&E—Fuel
Oil—Lubricants	Golf Course Maint.—Gasoline & Lubricants
Oil Tank Insurance	FC&IT—Insurance
Office Supplies and Accessories	A&G—Operating Supplies & Equipment

P

Item	Classification
Pager—Rentable	All Departments—Equipment Rental
Pails	Food/Beverage/Overnight Rooms/ Locker Rooms—Operating Supplies
Paint Cleaners	FM&E—Painting & Decorating
Pamphlets—Educational or Instructional (for Employees)	All Departments—Professional Development
Paper Bags	Food/Beverage—Operating Supplies
Paper Clips	A&G—Operating Supplies & Equipment; All Other Departments—Operating Supplies
Paper Napkins	Overnight Rooms/Food/Beverage— Operating Supplies
Paper Pads (Employee)	Overnight Rooms/Food/Beverage/ A&G—Printing & Stationery
Pastry Bags	Food—Operating Supplies
Payroll and Tax Forms	A&G—Printing & Stationery
Pencil Sharpeners	A&G—Operating Supplies and Equipment; Overnight Rooms/Food/Beverage— Operating Supplies
Pens and Pencils (Employees)	A&G—Operating Supplies and Equipment; Overnight Rooms/Food/Beverage— Operating Supplies
Pens and Pencils (Members and Guests)	Food/Beverage—Operating Supplies; Overnight Rooms—Member and Guest Supplies; Clubhouse—Member Supplies
Pencils—Golf	Golf Ops.—Operating Supplies
Pensions	All Departments—PT&EB
Personnel Forms	A&G—Printing & Stationery
Pest Control	FM&E—Pest Control
Petty Cash Forms	A&G—Printing & Stationery; Clubhouse— Operating Supplies
Physicians' Fees (Employees)	All Departments—PT&EB
Piano Rental	Clubhouse/Food/Beverage/ Entertainment—Equipment Rental
Pins (Employee)	All Departments—Uniforms
Pins (Flagsticks)	Golf Course Maint.—Operating Supplies
Pitchers	Food/Beverage—China

Item	Classification
Plaster Repairs	FM&E—Building
Plates—China	Food/Beverage—China
Plates—Paper	Food/Beverage—Operating Supplies
Platters	Food/Beverage—China
Playing Cards	Overnight Rooms—Member and Guest Supplies; Locker Rooms/Clubhouse—Member Supplies
Plumbing Repairs	FM&E—Plumbing
Polishes	Food/Beverage/Overnight Rooms—Operating Supplies
Pool—Accessories	Aquatic Sports—Operating Supplies
Pool—Chemicals	Aquatic Sports—Chemicals
Pool—Maintenance and Repairs	Aquatic Sports—Equipment Repair & Maint.
Post Office Box Rental	A&G—Postage
Postage	A&G—Postage
Postage for Promotional Mailings	A&G—Other Operating Expenses
Postage Meter Rentals	A&G—Equipment Rental
Posters—Safety	All Departments—Other Operating Expenses
Presentation Binders	A&G—Printing & Stationery
Printed Forms	All Departments—Printing & Stationery
Printer Supplies and Accessories	All Departments—Computer Expense
Prizes—Employee	All Departments—PT&EB
Professional Entertainers	Food/Beverage—Music & Entertainment; Entertainment—Contract Entertainment
Programs	A&G—Club Publications; Entertainment—Other Operating Expenses
Protective Service	Clubhouse—Security
Protest Fees	A&G—Professional Fees
Provision for Doubtful Accounts	A&G—Provision for Doubtful Accounts
Public Liability Insurance	FC&IT—Insurance—Liability
Pump Repairs	FM&E—Plumbing

R

Item	Classification
Rack Cards	Overnight Rooms—Printing & Stationery
Ramekins	Food—China
Real Estate Rent (Land and Buildings)	FC&IT—Rent
Real Estate Taxes	FC&IT—Real Estate Taxes
Recorders—Mini/Micro Cassette and Accessories	A&G—Operating Supplies & Equipment; Clubhouse—Operating Supplies
Recycle Bins	FM&E—Refuse Removal
Refrigeration Supplies	FM&E/Food/Beverage—Operating Supplies
Refuse Removal	FM&E—Refuse Removal
Registration Cards	Overnight Rooms—Printing & Stationery
Rent—Building and Land	FC&IT—Rent—Land & Buildings
Rent—Computer Equipment	All Departments—Computer Expense

Item	Classification
Rentals—Furniture & Equipment	All Departments—Equipment Rental
Reports and Report Covers	A&G—Printing & Stationery
Reservation Cards—Dining Room Tables . .	Food—Printing & Stationery
Reservation Forms	Overnight Rooms—Printing & Stationery
Restaurant Checks	Food/Beverage—Printing & Stationery
Restaurant Signs	Food—Operating Supplies
Ribbons—Typewriter, Printing Calculator Cash Register	A&G—Operating Supplies & Equipment
Royalties	Food/Beverage—Music & Entertainment; Entertainment—Royalties
Rubber Stamps	A&G—Operating Supplies & Equipment; All Other Departments—Operating Supplies

S

Item	Classification
Safe Deposit Box Keys	Overnight Rooms—Operating Supplies
Safe Deposit Box Rentals (Off-site)	A&G—Other
Sand—Bunkers/Traps	Golf Course Maint.—Sand & Top Dressing
Sand—Clubhouse/Grounds Use	FM&E—Grounds & Landscaping
Saucers	Overnight Rooms/Food/Beverage—China
Scissors and Scotch Tape	A&G—Operating Supplies & Equipment; All Other Departments—Operating Supplies
Security—Contracted	Clubhouse—Security
Service Manuals (Employee)	All Departments—Professional Development
Shampoo	Locker Rooms—Member Supplies; Overnight Rooms—Member & Guest Supplies; Health & Fitness/ Aquatic Sports/Racquet Sports— Operating Supplies
Sheet Music	Food/Beverage—Music & Entertainment; Entertainment—Other Operating Expenses
Sheets—Linen	Overnight Rooms—Laundry & Linen
Shoe Cloths	Overnight Rooms—Member & Guest Supplies
Signature Books	Clubhouse/Food/Beverage—Printing & Stationery
Silver Cleaners	Food/Beverage—Operating Supplies
Soap Powders	Clubhouse/Locker Rooms/Food/ Beverage—Operating Supplies— Cleaning Supplies
Soaps—Guest Room	Overnight Rooms—Member & Guest Supplies
Soaps—Locker and Fitness Facility	Health & Fitness—Operating Supplies; Locker Rooms—Member Supplies

Item	Classification
Social and Sports Activities—Employees ...	All Departments—PT&EB
Software—Application Upgrades	All Departments—Computer Expense
Software Leases	All Departments—Computer Expense
Soufflé Cups	Food—Operating Supplies
Souvenirs	Food/Beverage—Operating Supplies; Overnight Rooms—Member & Guest Supplies
Spoons...............................	Food/Beverage—China
Sports Activities and Equipment— Employees	All Departments—PT&EB
Stairway Repairs	FM&E—Building
Stamp Pads	A&G—Operating Expenses & Equipment; All Other Departments—Operating Supplies
Stamps—General	A&G—Postage
Staplers/Staples	A&G—Operating Supplies & Equipment; All Other Departments—Operating Supplies
State Income Taxes	FC&IT—State Income Tax
State Unemployment Taxes	All Departments—PT&EB
Stationery	A&G/Clubhouse—Printing & Stationery
Stationery (Guest)	Overnight Rooms—Member & Guest Supplies; Clubhouse—Member Supplies
Sticks—Swizzle; Stirrers	Food/Beverage—Operating Supplies
Stock Transfer Agents; Fees	A&G—Professional Fees
Storage Files	A&G—Operating Supplies & Equipment
Storage of Equipment/Records (Off-site) ..	A&G—Other Operating Expenses
Storeroom Issue Reports and Orders	Food/Beverage—Printing & Stationery
Strainers—Beverages	Beverage—Operating Supplies
Straws	Food/Beverage—Operating Supplies
Subscriptions—Trade Publications	All Departments—Dues & Subscriptions
Surge Protectors	All Departments—Computer Expense
Sweepers—Carpet	Clubhouse/Overnight Rooms/Food/ Beverage—Operating Supplies
Swim Suit Bags	Locker Rooms—Operating Supplies
Swimming Pool Repairs	Aquatic Sports—Equipment Repair & Maint.

T

Item	Classification
Table Cloths/Protectors/Tops	Food/Beverage—Laundry & Linen
Table Covers	Food/Beverage—Operating Supplies
Table Tent Cards	Food/Beverage—Printing & Stationery
Tags—Baggage	Overnight Rooms—Printing & Stationery
Tags—Laundry	House Laundry—Laundry Supplies
Tape	FM&E—Operating Supplies
Tape—Carpet	FM&E—Floor Coverings
Tape Recorders and Supplies	A&G—Operating Supplies & Equipment; Clubhouse—Operating Supplies

Item	Classification
Taxes—Beverage—State (Not Included in Purchase Price)	Beverage—Cost of Beverage
Taxicab Fares	All Departments—Other Operating Expenses
Teapots	Food/Beverage—China
Technical Books	All Departments—Professional Development
Tees—Golf	Golf Ops.—Operating Supplies
Telephone Accessories—General	A&G—Telephone
Telephone Charges	All Departments—Telephone
Telephone Directory Covers and Holders ..	Clubhouse/Overnight Rooms— Operating Supplies
Telephone Lines—Computer Rentals	A&G—Computer Expense
Telephone Rentals	Clubhouse/A&G—Equipment Rental; Telecommunications—Cost of Calls— Rental of Equipment
Television Rentals	All Departments—Equipment Rental
Temporary Help	All Departments—Salaries & Wages
Thread and Needles (Guest)	Locker—Member Supplies; Overnight Rooms—Member & Guest Supplies
Toner (for Copier)	A&G/Clubhouse—Printing & Stationery
Total Quality Management	All Departments—Professional Development
Towels	Clubhouse/Locker/Food/Beverage/ Aquatic Sports—Laundry & Linen
Trade Magazines and Publications Subscriptions	All Departments—Dues & Subscriptions
Transfer Fees	A&G—Professional Fees
Transportation of Employees	All Departments—Other Operating Expenses
Traveling Expenses	All Departments—Other Operating Expenses
Trays	Food/Beverage—China
Tumblers	Food/Beverage—China

U

Item	Classification
Uncollectible Accounts	A&G—Provision for Doubtful Accounts
Uniforms and Uniform Repair	All Departments—Uniforms
Union (Trade) Insurance and Pension Fund (Employer's Contribution)	All Departments—PT&EB
Utensils	Food/Beverage—Operating Supplies

V

Item	Classification
Vacuum Cleaner Accessories	Clubhouse/Locker/Overnight Rooms— Operating Supplies
Visual Planners	A&G—Operating Supplies & Equipment
Vouchers	A&G/Overnight Rooms/Food/Beverage— Printing & Stationery

Item	Classification

W

Item	Classification
Want Ads (Help Wanted)	All Departments—Other Operating Expenses
Wastebaskets (Employee)	A&G—Operating Supplies & Equipment; Clubhouse—Operating Supplies
Water—Clubhouse	FM&E—Water
Water—Swimming Pool	Aquatic Sports—Water
Water—Golf Course	Golf Course Maint.—Water
Wax Paper	Food/Beverage—Operating Supplies— Paper Supplies
Website Contract Service	A&G—Website Development & Maint.
Website Hosting Fee	A&G—Website Development & Maint.
Website Software	A&G—Website Development & Maint.
Weather Systems—Leased Equipment (Operating Lease)	Golf Ops.—Equipment Rental
Window Shades—Contract Cleaning	Various Departments—Contract Services
Window Shades, Screen, and Awning Repairs	FM&E—Curtains & Draperies
Wine Baskets	Beverage—Operating Supplies
Wine Lists	Beverage—Operating Supplies
Wired Music—Dining Rooms	Food/Beverage—Music & Entertainment
Wired Music—Lobby	Clubhouse—Other Operating Expenses
Workers' Compensation Insurance	All Departments—PT&EB
Wrapping Paper (Laundry)	House Laundry—Laundry Supplies
Wrapping Paper and Twine	Overnight Rooms—Operating Supplies
Writing Supplies—Overnight Rooms	Overnight Rooms—Member & Guest Supplies